Wine Country COOKING

FROM

GLENORA
WINE CELLARS

IN THE HEART OF
THE FINGER LAKES WINE REGION

COPYRIGHT NOTICE

WINE COUNTRY COOKING
from Glenora Wine Cellars

is published by
SIDE ORDER BOOKS
(www.sideorderbooks.com)

Book Design: Anne Kiley
Illustrations: William Benson
Cover Photography: Kristian S. Reynolds
Project Editors: Thomas Pellechia and Michael Turback

ISBN: 978-0-9787368-7-3

Printed in the United States of America

This book is dedicated to all who love wine and food,
and to all who visit the Finger Lakes region
to enjoy them.

TABLE OF CONTENTS

White Wines and Recipes

Red Wines and Recipes

Special Occasion Wines and Recipes

Picnic Wines and Recipes

INTRODUCTION

It all started in the Finger Lakes around 1830, when a minister named William Bostwick arrived and planted the first grape vines in the region. The good reverend procured those grapevine cuttings from the already active wine region in New York's Hudson Valley.

He planted his vines in Hammondsport, at the southern end of Keuka Lake, and that is where a local wine industry began in 1858.

Known for its cool and often erratic climate, the Finger Lakes region at first produced its best wines from so-called Native American grapes—many of the local grape varieties are the result of spontaneous field crosses between Native American grapes and European grapes that settlers brought with them to the New World. Two of the most famous grape varieties from the Finger Lakes wine industry of the past, Catawba and Isabella, were discovered growing in the Carolinas in the early 19th century.

Because of the weather, it took 100 years before the Finger Lakes region was able to successfully grow and produce wine from the more tender European grape varieties like Riesling, Gewurztraminer, Pinot Blanc, Chardonnay, Pinot Noir, and Cabernet Franc. But after that, what had already been known as a vibrant and premium local wine region was quickly revolutionized into a world-class competitor—it took only thirty years from the first commercial local Riesling to reach the heights.

One year following the passage in New York of the Farm Winery Act in 1976, along with Howard Kimball, three eminent Seneca Lake grape growers,

Ed Dalrymple, Eastman Beers, and Gene Pierce created Glenora Wine Cellars, with Pierce leading the way; as a young man, he had studied agricultural economics at Cornell University.

At the time, Keuka Lake was still the Finger Lakes industry's center of gravity, but Glenora Wine Cellars was established at Seneca Lake, some 30 miles east of Keuka. Like the initial wine revolution, it didn't take long for Seneca Lake to become the center of the Finger Lakes wine world, and Glenora was in the forefront of that shift, with Pierce at the helm, where he remains today.

The first Glenora winemaker, New York native John Williams, was trained at the University of California, Davis Campus and in the famous Napa Valley winery, Stags Leap. The partners at Glenora reasoned that a California-trained winemaker would jump start the small Finger Lakes wine industry that had set its sights on competing nationally and internationally. The winery hosted a few more winemakers over the years, from California and locally, before settling on the multi-talented and well trained Steve DiFrancesco.

The aim at Glenora has always been to produce wine that directly reflects the local "terroir," that mystical notion that says a wine's character comes from that vineyard's unique place on the globe. Whether the wines are produced from the classic European grape varieties or from New World varieties, the soul of Glenora wine is 100% Finger Lakes, broken down into the macroclimate of the appellation and the specific mesoclimates of the various vineyards and microclimates of specific vineyard rows.

The hallmark of Glenora wine is its aromatic intensity and bright, vibrant mouth-feel wine that demands a good meal right beside it. That's why, in the late 1980s, responding to visitors' desire for a solid local restaurant, Pierce and partners invested in their next adventure, the addition of a restaurant attached to the winery tasting room.

At first, the restaurant was a casual affair. But as time went by, Pierce heard one too many times from tourists seeking fine accommodations for an extended stay plus top-notch sustenance. In 1999, Glenora erected a 30-room luxury inn complete with a top-level restaurant: the Inn at Glenora Wine Cellars and Veraisons Restaurant.

Visitors voted with their reservations. The success of the inn led to an extension known as "the cottage," located just down the slope from the inn, toward Seneca Lake—it's for those seeking a home away from home.

The inn and restaurant have become not only a stop on the Seneca wine tour but also a place for weddings, conferences and local family gatherings. And speaking of local, just as it is with Glenora wines being the result of grapes grown in the surroundings, Veraisons Restaurant places much value on procuring ingredients from local produce and livestock sources.

This book is the culmination of years of Glenora Wine Cellars experience in wine, food, and hospitality. It is our way of showing you what you can do at home to replicate what we are always ready to do for you at our home.

TWO GENTLEMEN OF GLENORA

The job of a winemaker isn't always to make wine, and an executive chef isn't always behind a stove.

While it takes years of study to become either a competent winemaker or chef, it takes immeasurable hard work to become the boss, the one who not only has the expertise and the vision but also the management capability.

To keep up the high quality means that Steve Di Francesco, our winemaker, must oversee nearly 115,000 gallons of wine and a wine production staff of no fewer than three full-time and up to six part-time employees. He must also satisfy a number of local and federal agencies with monthly reports, coordinate with the production manager wine releases so that they are timed not to interrupt the inventory flow, make himself available for winery promotion events where he pours and talks about wine, and participate in many wine seminars and give speeches.

Steve made his way to the position of head winemaker by first becoming a microbiologist, earning a degree at Stetson University in DeLand, Florida; then, he landed in the Finger Lakes region in 1979, as assistant to Guy DeVaux and Charles Fournier in their sparkling wine production at the venerable but now gone Gold Seal Vineyards. He went on to work at two more wineries, each time working his way up the responsibility ladder, before settling at Glenora Wine Cellars in 1995, as chief winemaker.

Steve is a fanatic about attention to detail. He has to be. He not only heads Glenora's winemaking but he also oversees winemaking at the sister winery,

Knapp Vineyards on Cayuga Lake.

At Glenora, Steve's steady hand and full attention to detail shines through in the award-winning production of classical Méthode Champenoise sparkling wine. But that's not all. His talent spreads into the production of still table wines, especially with the Finger Lakes regions' premium grape variety, Riesling, but also with many of the uncommon grape varieties that the winery either grows or buys from local growers, varieties like Pinot Blanc, Gewurztraminer, Syrah, Merlot (the latter two are red grapes that aren't supposed to do well in the cool northeast).

As Executive Chef, Orlando Rodriguez creates recipes, cultivates sources of local foods, keeps a watchful eye on food costs and waste, oversees a kitchen staff of six full-time and up to six part-time, lends a hand managing the wait staff, steps out front of the kitchen to meet the customers at special dinners and on special dining evenings, and is an overall ambassador for quality at both Veraisons Restaurant and at the Inn At Glenora Wine Cellars.

A New England native of Dominican heritage, Chef Orlando grew up in Danbury, Connecticut. His early interest in cooking led him to attend the renowned Culinary Institute of America in Hyde Park, New York.

After graduating with skill in classroom cooking, Orlando went home to Connecticut to start a career.

To be a chef is to be an apprentice first. There's probably no way around it. So, for the next ten years Orlando apprenticed, picking up invaluable hands-on culinary lessons and inspirations in Connecticut with two of the country's top chefs, first with the award-winning Chef Brendan Walsh at the Elms Restaurant & Tavern, in Ridgefield; then, with Chef Albert DeAngelis at Mediterraneo, in Greenwich.

Ready to make his own mark in the kitchen, Orlando discovered the intriguing wealth of local produce and wines in New York's Finger Lakes region after meeting with Glenora Wine Cellars President, Gene Pierce, late in 2007. The following year, he accepted the challenge of his first take-charge position to bring his striking clarity and quality of simplicity as the chef at Veraisons Restaurant at the Inn at Glenora Wine Cellars.

Today, Executive Chef Orlando Rodriguez combines his talent for sophisticated American cuisine with local and regional nuances, creating a uniquely exquisite form of wine country fare, allowing the region's bounty to shine through in every entrée, without fuss or overbearing technique.

In addition to their regular responsibilities, Steve and Orlando spend time together talking over how best to pair Glenora wines with Veraison recipes. Those conversations are the basis for this cookbook, so as you read this book you'll be eavesdropping. Doesn't that sound like fun?

WINERY
RESTAURANT

White Wines
and Recipes

Cayuga White

It goes without saying, but we'll say it anyway: the aim of a winemaker in a region known for its aromatic grape varieties, is to produce wines that are an appropriate accompaniment to a meal. That's why winemaker, Steve DiFrancesco, has a particular passion for Cayuga White.

The result of a cross between the French-American hybrid, Seyval (see page 19) and a local hybrid, Schuyler, Cayuga White is the first highly successful wine grape hybrid to be created at the Cornell University Agricultural Station in Geneva, New York. Work on the grape started in the mid 1940s, but since it requires painstaking vineyard and wine trials before a new variety enters the commercial world, Cayuga White was released in 1972 for winemaking in cool climate grape regions.

A local wine writer once referred to Cayuga White as the Chenin Blanc of the Finger Lakes, and rightly so. Considerable European "blood" runs through the grape variety's veins, as both Seyval and Schuyler are hybrid crosses of European and Native American varieties. Cayuga White is fruity, crisp, and overall light bodied yet quite food friendly, just like the Chenin Blanc of France's cool Loire region.

If all goes well, Cayuga White is ready to pick by the last week of September. But with nature, all doesn't often go well. As the month of September rolls in, Steve begins to walk the Cayuga vineyards nearby to follow the ripening path of the grapes. This quite fruity variety can take on a bitter component if left on the vines for too long after ripening. Steve's aim is to harvest the grapes when they are at their fruitiest and their most aromatic. At that point, Cayuga White grapes are also crisply acidic.

We produce four separate wines from Cayuga White grapes, three of which are blends with Cayuga as their base. The fourth wine is 100% Cayuga White. The aroma of this last wine is a mystical mix of tropical fruits and citrus. With a little residual sugar in the finished wine, the taste is a tingling and pleasant balance between fruit, sugar, light alcohol, and bracing, snappy acidity. In other words, Cayuga White wine is ready to stand up to all kinds of foods, especially those with a strong presence of their own like venison, wild turkey, salmon, shellfish, and for the meatless among us, vegetables with uncommon power, like asparagus and Brussels sprouts.

Glenora Wine Cellars was the first winery in the U.S. to release a varietal Cayuga White; the grape has been a standard Finger Lakes wine ever since.

Seared Yellow Fin Tuna with Citrus Salad

The rich flavor and texture of seared tuna provide the centerpiece to this refreshing appetizer, and citrus fruits give the dish an intriguing contrast of flavors. Quick to prepare, this dish will definitely be a talking point when you have guests for dinner.

Ingredients:

- 1 pound yellow fin tuna, cut into 4-ounce portions
- 2 oranges, peeled and segmented
- 2 lemons, peeled and segmented
- 2 limes, peeled and segmented
- 8 ounces mixed greens
- 1/4 cup lemon juice
- 3/4 cup olive oil
- To taste salt and pepper
- 1 tablespoon vegetable oil

Place a sauté pan on high heat on the stove top and add the vegetable oil. When the oil has produced a light smoke, place the tuna in the pan. Sear each side of the tuna for approximately one minute. Mix the lemon juice and olive oil for the dressing and reserve to the side. In a bowl, mix the segments of lime, lemon, oranges and mixed greens. Add about two tablespoon of the citrus dressing to the salad and mix. Place the mixture in the center of the plate. Slice tuna and arrange on top.

Makes four servings.

KITCHEN STORIES

Cayuga White adds a bit of the "exotic" to the dish with its soft, juicy fruitiness. It coats the palate and broadens the taste of the tuna, making a very successful match.

Sautéed Shrimp with Lemon-Caper Butter and Goat Cheese

The wine plays a different role in this dish than it does in the glass. Cayuga contributes depth, fragrance, sweetness, and tang as it contrasts it with semi-spicy notes of the butter for a yin-yang taste experience.

Cook pasta in six quarts of boiling water between seven to ten minutes. In a large sauté pan add the oil over medium-high heat. Add shrimp and cook for about two minutes on each side. Add garlic, capers, and thyme; cook for about two minutes. Add the Cayuga wine to deglaze the pan and cook for an additional three minutes. Stir in the butter until melted, then add the tomatoes and pasta. To finish, crumble goat cheese over the top.

Makes four servings.

Ingredients:

1-1/2 pounds shrimp, medium-size, peeled and deveined
3/4 pound angel hair pasta
2 tablespoons virgin olive oil
1/2 pound butter
1 tablespoon garlic, minced
1 teaspoon thyme leaves, fresh
2 tablespoon capers
4 vine-ripened tomatoes, diced
1/3 cup Glenora Cayuga White
1/2 pound goat cheese

Lively Run Goat Dairy in nearby Interlaken is our source for a mild, fresh, "user friendly" goat cheese that melts on this dish like a ripe brie.

Grilled Soy-Marinated Venison Loin

Cayuga may be a white wine, but Finger Lakes hunters love to pair venison with the complex fruit and liveliness of this regional hybrid, both to improve the texture and to take that gamey taste out of game hunted in the wild. Fire up the charcoal grill to medium-high heat. Grill until crunchy on the outside, tender inside.

Ingredients:

1-1/2 pounds venison loin
1/4 cup soy sauce
1 teaspoon sesame oil
1/4 cup vegetable oil
1 teaspoon garlic, minced

Combine the soy sauce, sesame oil, vegetable oil, and garlic. Add in the venison loin and marinate for about two hours in the refrigerator. Remove venison from refrigerator and return to room temperature before cooking. Grill for about four minutes on each side. To serve, slice the loin on the diagonal.

Makes four servings.

Keep in mind the fact that with a good bottle of Cayuga, you can toss out the rulebook that says "red wine with meat."

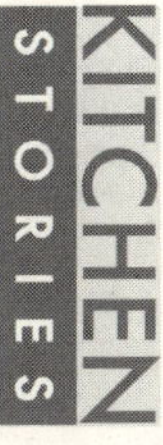

Sesame Green Beans with Toasted Almonds

For such a simple dish, you will be surprised at the delightful flavor, as sesame oil perfumes the air and gives the beans a light nutty flavor. Sesame oil is a great pantry investment as a tiny amount can add so much flavor to stir-fry, soups, and salads. Chinese long beans cut into smaller lengths also work well in this recipe.

Ingredients:

- 1 pound green beans
- 1/4 cup toasted almonds
- 1 tablespoon soy sauce
- 1/4 teaspoon sesame oil

Warm a large skillet or wok over medium heat. When the skillet is hot, pour in sesame oil, then place green beans into the skillet. Stir the beans to coat with oil. Cook until the beans are bright green and slightly browned in spots, about four minutes. Remove from heat, and stir in soy sauce; cover, and let sit about five minutes. Transfer to a serving platter, and sprinkle with toasted almonds.

Makes four servings.

The toasted almonds add a little extra crunch and pop with toasty goodness when you bite into the beans.

Crème Caramel

Dessert and wine pairings can be tricky. With that in mind, a crème caramel with subdued sweetness becomes an attractive partner with Cayuga White. The addition of fresh berries will turn this from a complementary pairing to a more nuanced match, revealing surprise flavors of peach and stone fruit in the wine.

Ingredients:
- 3 eggs, whole
- 3 eggs, whites
- 3/4 cup sugar (for cream)
- 2 cup heavy cream
- 1 vanilla bean
- 1 cups sugar (for caramel)

Step 1: place sugar for caramel in a sauce pan and cook at a medium heat till the sugar melts and its color becomes amber. Place the caramel into six individual three-ounce ramekins (just enough to coat the bottom of the ramekin). Set to the side and let cool.

Step 2: place heavy cream, sugar, vanilla bean split and scraped into a sauce pan. Bring to a boil. Once the cream mixture has come to a boil, add two ounces of the hot liquid to the mixture of egg whites and whole eggs and combine with a whisk. Once incorporated, continue adding the hot liquid, two ounces at a time, until completely incorporated. Strain mixture.

Step 3: place the mixture inside the ramekins with the caramel. Place ramekins inside a shallow pan, with water covering half of the ramekins to create a water bath. Place in oven for ninety minutes at 325 degrees. Remove from oven and let cool overnight in refrigerator. When ready to serve, run a small knife along the edge of the custard and allow custard to fall out of ramekin onto serving plate.

Makes six servings.

KITCHEN STORIES

As a general rule, dessert shouldn't be sweeter than the accompanying wine, lest it overpower the drink.

Seyval Blanc

Not every winery produces Seyval; but don't hold that against them; they probably don't know what they are missing.

This French-American white hybrid grape produces the closest thing to the Old World (European) style wine than just about any other hybrid grown in the New World (American) style wine.

Seyval made it to the Finger Lakes region by way of Europe and then Maryland, where grape grower Philip Wagner planted the vine, and the idea that it was well suited for Mid-Atlantic and Northeastern climates.

The Seyval grapes we use are grown at Glenora Farms, right outside and across the road from the winery. As a hybrid, Seyval withstands the vagaries of Finger Lakes weather more easily than its European neighbors located in separate plots of the same vineyard, proving that Mr. Wagner was correct.

Some say that Seyval wine reminds very much of Sauvignon Blanc; perhaps, but others say it reminds of Chardonnay. On its own, with minimal winemaker intervention, Seyval is indeed reminiscent of the former. Let it ferment and then age in premium oak barrels, and yes, there is a resemblance to the latter. But like every wine, Seyval has both its own identity plus the stamp of the wine producer.

Steve's version of Seyval offers a marvelous sensory stimulation that begins with grassy, earthy aromas and ends with a snapping, crisp, lemony finish. In between, Steve's judicious use of fermentation in oak barrels tones down the wine's somewhat raciness so that it feels richer and fuller than a stainless steel treatment, alone, would provide.

Its earthy freshness and citrus-like character make our Seyval a natural for seafood, Cornish hens, and soft, creamy cheeses.

WINE CELLAR STORIES

Seyval was hybridized in France in the 19th century, in the search for a cure to a root disease that was wiping out France's vineyards. It became the darling of many French winemakers, but in the 1960s, the grape was uprooted, as it was not a "natural" Old World vine.

Cornmeal-Crusted Fried Calamari

It's the Italian word for squid, and its sweet-tasting, firm-textured meat has been lovingly appropriated in New World cuisine. In this preparation, sweet, nutty cornmeal coating is light and not overbearing, maintaining the integrity of the natural calamari flavor, while a simple splash of fresh lemon juice connects the dish to citrus notes in the Seyval Blanc.

Ingredients:

1-1/2 pounds squid, cut in quarter-inch thick rounds
2 ounces milk
1/2 cup cornmeal
1/2 cup all purpose flour
1 teaspoon fresh parsley
1 lemon

In a bowl, mix calamari and milk together. Drain excess liquid. Blend together the cornmeal and flour. Add the calamari to the mixture and toss until well coated. Fry calamari at 325 degrees in a fryer until golden brown, about three to five minutes. (Don't overcook or it will be very rubbery). Remove the calamari from the deep fryer with a slotted spoon. Drain on paper towels. Season with salt and pepper. Garnish with fresh parsley and squeeze fresh lemon juice over top.

Makes four servings.

The squid you buy will likely be frozen or previously frozen. Look for flesh that's shiny ivory, overlaid with tasteful speckles. The body becomes the squid tube; separate the tentacles and slice into those characteristic calamari rings.

Mussels Steamed in Seyval Blanc

There's no better way to cook mussels than steaming, and Seyval Blanc adds a special touch to this classic Belgian dish. Steaming opens up the shells to release flavorful juices that drip down to the bottom of the pot and combine with the garlic and butter-enriched liquid to become a flavorful, aromatic broth. For authenticity, serve with a pile of french fries and mayonnaise.

Ingredients:

2 pounds mussels, de-bearded and washed
4 vine ripe tomatoes, seeded and diced medium
1 teaspoon garlic minced
1 cup Glenora Seyval Blanc
1 tablespoon olive oil
1 bunch parlsey, rough chop
To taste salt
To taste ground black pepper
1 lemon, juiced
3 tablespoons butter

In a medium sauté skillet over medium-high heat, add butter, and lightly toast the garlic and shallots. Add mussels and wine. Cover and cook for about ten to fifteen minutes or until mussels steam open. Add tomatoes, parsley, lemon juice and butter. Salt and pepper to taste.

Makes four servings.

Go ahead, eat with your hands. Pick up each shell in your fingers and eat, sopping up the abundant, buttery broth with some crusty French bread as you go. Hunt through the shells to make sure you've found every last morsel.

Grilled Red Snapper with Strawberry Salsa

Nothing captures the essence of summer days like fresh fish prepared and eaten outdoors, served with a fruity, flavorful wine. The exalted red snapper has a lean, firm texture that is perfect for grilling. Sear the fillets, creating a sort of crust that will separate easily from the grill (moving the fish too soon will encourage sticking). To flip fish, slide a large spatula along the lines of the grill and then carefully roll the fish piece over to finish cooking. The surprising combination of a sweet and spicy salsa provides a delightful foil to the delicately flavored snapper.

Ingredients:

4 6-ounce red snapper fillets
2 tablespoons olive oil
1 teaspoon ground cumin
1 teaspoon garlic
1 lime, juiced
To taste salt
To taste ground black pepper

For the strawberry salsa:

1/2 pint strawberries, diced
1 jalapeno, minced
2 limes, juiced
1 lemon, zest
1 small red onion, finely diced
1 tablespoon cilantro, chopped finely
1 pinch salt

To make the fish: combine the olive oil, cumin, garlic, lime juice, salt and pepper rub on the outside of the fillet. Grill for about four minutes on each side over medium-high heat. (Be sure to oil grate so fish doesn't stick).

To make the salsa: combine all ingredients together and toss well. Serve salsa over the grilled red snapper.

Makes four servings.

Strawberry season in the Finger Lakes is short, so we treasure ours with a bountiful harvest of Early Glow, which sets and ripens by mid-June: so big and juicy you can almost eat them out of hand like a peach.

Citrus-Rubbed Roasted Chicken

The green pastures of Evergreen Farm in Rock Stream, just two miles from the winery, are home to free-ranging chickens, fed with whole organic grains and pure spring water. Seyval Blanc meets its perfect match with these healthy, lean birds, prepared with a simple lemon-based rub to avoid overpowering their succulent, naturally rich flavor.

Ingredients:

1 3-1/2 pound chicken
2 lemons, juiced and zest of one
1 tablespoon fresh thyme leaves
1 tablespoon parsley, finely chopped
2 cloves garlic, mashed
1 tablespoon kosher salt
1 teaspoon black pepper
1 tablespoon olive oil
1 teaspoon cumin, ground

Pre-heat oven to 325 degrees. Trim any excess skin from the chicken and remove the gizzards and neck and discard. Mix together in a small bowl the lemon juice, lemon zest, thyme, parsley, garlic, salt, pepper, olive oil and cumin, and rub on the outside of the chicken. Place chicken in a roasting pan and roast for one hour and fifteen minutes, or until internal temperature reaches 165 degrees. Remove from the oven and let rest for fifteen minutes before serving.

Makes four servings.

KITCHEN STORIES

Lean, free-range meat means that slower cooking yields better results. Slow and low roasting brings out more abundant, natural flavor, and basting improves tenderness.

Wilted Spinach with Sautéed Shallots

An easy and delicious side dish, all it requires is a bunch of fresh spinach, some shallots, olive oil, and a sauté pan. Fruity olive oil coats the leaves, with a splash of water to braise the greens. For a special treat, use Bloomsdale or one of the other heirloom varieties. Just remember to wilt the spinach quickly, taking care not to overcook. Shallots add an intriguing, faint onion flavor.

Ingredients:

8 ounces baby spinach
1 tablespoon shallots, minced
1 tablespoon olive oil
1 tablespoon butter, unsalted
2 tablespoons water
1/4 teaspoon ground black pepper
1 teaspoon salt

In a large sauté pan add olive oil, and shallots. Cook for about three minutes, then add butter salt, pepper, and water. Add the baby spinach and cook until wilted.

Makes four servings.

Although France is the spiritual home of the shallot, this revered culinary ingredient was introduced to French kitchens by returning armies after the first Crusade. Researchers have traced its origins to Ascalom, the oldest and largest seaport of old Palestine.

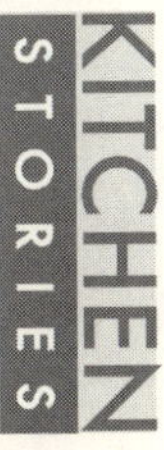

CHARDONNAY

To produce lush, almost tropical white wine in the Northeast requires a great white wine vineyard site. Steve is glad that we have one of those.

The 30 year-old Dalrymple Chardonnay vineyard is located close to Seneca Lake, on its east shore with full daily sun exposure, and in the heart of the so-called banana belt. The grapes from this vineyard are so site specific that it gave impetus to a new program at the winery for Vineyard Designated wines that will sport the name of the vineyard on the labels of wines with special site-specific qualities.

Steve feels that Chardonnay is the most "abused wine on the planet."

What he means is that this is the one white grape that winemakers can't seem to leave alone. They almost treat it as if it were a red grape, shooting for opulence and oakiness.

Steve's plan is to highlight the variety's natural fruitiness as well as those vineyard site-specific qualities, which in the banana belt are almost like tropical fruit: you can feel the palm trees sway, hear the pineapples fall from the trees, and taste lush mango-like fruit.

But Steve doesn't stop there. He also takes in Chardonnay from Glenora Farms vineyards and from Norbud Farm, a long-standing local fruit and dairy establishment owned by Ryan Bossert that was turned into vineyards at the turn of the 21st century. Exposed to less sunshine than the Dalrymple site, the Chardonnay grapes from Norbud provide crisp apple-like qualities, so our Chardonnay comes in two styles.

The crisp, racy style produced strictly in stainless steel tanks emphasizes the apple-like Chardonnay fruit, and the softer quieter style produced from malolactic fermentation (a secondary fermentation to convert malic into softer lactic acid) that is better suited to the tropical Chardonnay.

With seafood and poultry, definitely Chardonnay. But don't rule out topping your dishes with a creamy sauce, something that Chardonnay welcomes gladly and rewards stupendously.

WINE CELLAR STORIES

Chardonnay is one of the most widely planted white wine grapes in the world. It is the rare wine grape that adapts to just about any grape growing climate. At one time, it was the largest selling wine of any color in the United States.

Red Buddy-Crusted Onion Soup

Caramelized sweet onions swim in rich beef stock, smothered with melted cheese over toasted slabs of French bread. This hearty soup, enhanced with spunky garlic, becomes the perfect antidote to a long Finger Lakes winter, and each spoonful oozes with "Red Buddy," a cross of Swiss and Gouda style cheeses. A herd of contented Holsteins at Muranda Farms in nearby Waterloo provide the milk for the production of this local cheese.

Ingredients:

- 3 pounds sweet onions
- 1/2 cup fresh thyme leaves
- 1 each bay leaf
- 6 each minced garlic
- 2 ounces olive oil
- 1-1/2 quarts beef stock
- 1 baguette, sliced half-inch thick
- 6 ounces Red Buddy cheese (substitute: Swiss or Gouda)

In a medium sauce pan, add the olive oil and onion and cook over medium heat covered for about twenty minutes. Once it has become translucent, turn up heat, uncover and cook until golden in color. (Stir onions occasionally so they do not stick). Once the color is achieved, add thyme, bay leaf, garlic, and chicken stock. Simmer soup for thirty minutes. Portion into desired serving container and place baguette and shredded cheese on top, then place in a 400-degree oven for ten minutes or until cheese is melted.

Makes six servings.

The "black dirt" of New York's Orange County is perfect for growing sweet onions. The soil's high sulfur content provides an important component in the flavor profile of a good cooking onion. It's also what makes you cry when you are chopping them.

Capellini with Seared Sea Scallops

This recipe for sweet scallop morsels with Mediterranean-influenced flavors—trumpet mushrooms, kalamata olives, tomatoes, garlic and shallots—is best answered by the richness of a Chardonnay, creamy and buttery from its time in oak. The weightier wine forms a seamless bridge to the dish's silky textures and nutty, pan-browned flavors. Sea scallops are so tender that they cook quickly, and should always be patted dry before being added to the hot pan.

Ingredients:

3/4 pound capelinni pasta, cooked
20 sea scallop, large
4 ounces black trumpet mushrooms
1 cup kalamata olives, sliced and pitted
1/2 cup tomatoes, seeded and small diced
2 lemons, juiced
2 cup crème fraiche
1 tablespoon fresh thyme
To taste salt
To taste ground black pepper
1 teaspoon garlic, minced
1 tablespoon shallots, minced
1/2 cup Glenora Chardonnay

In a large saucier pan, sear scallops on one side for four minutes until golden brown, then remove from pan and set aside. Add garlic, shallots and mushroom and stir for two minutes, then deglaze with Glenora Chardonnay. Add olives, thyme, and crème fraiche and bring to a simmer. Add pasta and scallops, and season with salt and pepper. Finish with tomatoes and lemon juice.

Makes four servings.

Scallops are revered as aphrodisiacs, celebrated by Botticelli in his painting of Aphrodite, the goddess of love, standing on a scallop shell. The word aphrodisiac *comes from Aphrodite.*

Oven-Roasted Salmon with Cucumber Relish

Cooking salmon at a high temperature in the oven nicely browns the outside while assuring a moist, perfectly cooked inside. While salmon can stand perfectly well on its own, the easy, no-cook relish adds interesting flavors, crisp texture, and a little acidity to balance the richness of the fish, while an accompanying Chardonnay helps cut its natural oiliness. *Serve this dish in mid-summer, when local farmer's markets are brimming with heaps of slender, deep green cucumbers.*

Pre-heat oven to 400 degrees. Season salmon with salt and pepper. Add the olive oil to a sauté pan. Sear one side of the salmon, then place in oven for six minutes. Remove from the oven and serve with the relish.

Place all relish ingredients in a bowl and mix together and reserve. Once salmon is out of the oven, place relish over the fish and serve.

Makes four servings.

Ingredients:

4 6-ounce salmon fillets, preferably organic or wild
2 tablespoon olive oil
To taste salt
To taste ground black pepper

For the relish:

1 seedless cucumber, peeled and small diced
1/2 red onion, small diced
2 tablespoon white wine vinegar
1 tablespoon olive oil
1 teaspoon salt
1/2 teaspoon ground black pepper
1 teaspoon dill, finely chopped

Wild salmon are about thirty percent higher in Omega-3 fatty acid, a health-promoting fat which is one of the best reasons to eat salmon.

Pan-Seared Crab Cake with Garlic Tartar Sauce

Tall, golden cylinders of crab find a soul mate with a Chardonnay that has both the weight and complexity to stand up to the interplay of textures and flavors in this dish. Moist lump crabmeat, enclosed in a delicately crisp crust, is supported with restrained spices to enhance the flavor of the crab instead of disguising it. Fresh crab is already cooked, which means that the secondary cooking (or re-warming) must be done quickly to avoid drying the meat.

Ingredients:

- 2 limes (the zest of one and the juice of both)
- 1/3 cup breadcrumbs
- 1/4 teaspoon Old Bay seasoning
- 16 ounces fresh jumbo lump crabmeat, drained
- 1/2 teaspoon salt
- 1/4 teaspoon black pepper
- 2 tablespoon chives, finely chopped
- 1/2 cup mayonnaise
- 2 cups bread crumbs
- 1/4 cup vegetable oil

For the tartar sauce:

- 1/2 lemon
- 2 gherkins
- 1 small shallot
- 1 garlic clove
- 1 teaspoon capers
- 1 cup mayonnaise

Preheat oven to 400 degrees. Mix all ingredients together in a bowl, except the two cups of bread crumbs and oil. Portion crab into three ounce round balls, then gently flatten by hand into a patty. Coat the crab cakes with bread crumbs. Place oil in a sauté pan on medium-high heat. Sear one side of each crab cake for about four minutes or until golden brown. Flip over and place pan in oven for about ten minutes. Remove from oven and serve with tartar sauce.

For the tartar sauce: in a food processor, add juice of half a lemon, gherkins, half of the shallot, garlic, and caper. Pulse until finely chopped. Fold in mayonnaise and season with salt and pepper to taste.

Makes six servings.

No saltwater creature gives as much pleasure, profit, and good eating along North America's Atlantic and Gulf of Mexico coasts than the blue crab. The picked meat is hailed for its tenderness and sweet flavor.

Roasted Pork Loin with Chestnuts

Chestnuts ripen during the cooler months from September to November. Once they become fully developed, the nuts fall onto the ground for easy retrieval. In a dish with an especially winter feel, fresh chestnuts provide sweet, earthy counterpoint to the savory pork loin. To remove shells from fresh chestnuts, boil in water for a few minutes and then peel. It's important that the chestnuts stay hot while you're working, so you'll need to wear rubber gloves.

Combine the parsley, thyme, lemon zest, lemon juice, and season with salt and pepper. Cut the pork loin in the middle and stuff with the herb-lemon mixture, then tie together with butcher's twine. Rub the outside with salt, pepper and olive oil, place in roasting pan with the shallots, chestnuts, carrots, and garlic; roast in a 375-degree oven for one hour. Remove from oven and let rest for approximately fifteen minutes.

Makes four servings.

Ingredients:

1/2 cup breadcrumbs
1/2 cup chopped parsley
1 tablespoon fresh thyme leaves
1 lemon, juiced and zest
1 pork loin, bone in, 4 pounds
1/2 pound chestnuts, peeled
2 carrots, large dice
2 garlic cloves, thinly slice
6 shallots, halved
2 tablespoons olive oil
To taste salt
To taste ground black pepper

KITCHEN STORIES

Chestnut trees were once so numerous along the Eastern forests, it is said that a squirrel could jump from chestnut tree to chestnut tree all the way from Georgia to New York without ever touching the ground.

Oven-Roasted Cauliflower

Roasting on high heat deepens the sweet, nutty, comforting flavors of cauliflower. A generous squirt of lemon just before serving adds another dimension to the dish and establishes a connection to the crisp citrus notes in Chardonnay.

Ingredients:
1 head cauliflower
1/4 pound unsalted butter
To taste salt
To taste ground black pepper
2 tablespoon chopped parsley
Freshly squeezed lemon juice

Cut out the center of the cauliflower and separate the outer florets of the cauliflower. Pre-heat oven to 400 degrees. In a large sauté pan, melt butter then toss in the cauliflower. Cook on stove top until achieving a light golden color, then place in oven. Cook for fifteen minutes, then remove from oven, place in a platter, and sprinkle chopped parsley over the top. Finish with a squeeze of lemon juice.

Makes four servings.

Cauliflower prefers fertile, well drained soil rich in organic matter for best growth. Local cauliflower heads grown at Bauman Farms in nearby Webster often reach the size of basketballs.

Balsamic-Grilled Asparagus

Asparagus is one of the first vegetables ready to harvest in the spring, and aged balsamic lifts this early season side dish to new heights. A full-bodied, oaky Chardonnay flirts convincingly with both the energetic flavor of asparagus and the wine-friendly, sweet-tart flavor of balsamic vinegar.

Ingredients:

1 bunch asparagus
1 tablespoon olive oil
To taste salt
To taste ground black pepper
1 tablespoon aged balsamic vinegar

Mix all ingredients together. Place on grill at medium-high heat for about two minutes on each side.

Makes four servings.

KITCHEN STORIES

To make balsamic vinegar, Trebbiano grape pressings are boiled down to a dark syrup, then aged in wooden casks to add character to the vinegar. It's this aging process that makes true Italian balsamic so expensive. Luckily, a little goes a long way.

Dry Riesling

The first Riesling vines were planted in the Finger Lakes in the1950s—the first crop of wine was harvested in the 1960s, and the first Glenora Wine Cellars Riesling was produced in 1977.

Since the early days of Riesling, the domestic wine world has slowly but continuously been noticing the special and world class status of the variety in the Finger Lakes. Today, that notice is world-wide: Riesling isn't only the signature variety to the region's winemakers, it is recognized as ***the*** signature variety of the Finger Lakes.

Riesling is a consistent producer in the vineyard, in bad years and in good ones. But its special ability to express the qualities of its individual vineyard location makes this a variety of uncommon affinity with the earth. There is a definite reason that we have produced Riesling from the day we opened our doors for business.

Riesling needs no extended skin contact time, no oak barrels, no secondary fermentation, and no worrying in the middle of the night—all it asks is quiet stewardship. For our patient, watchful winemaker, Riesling rewards with the most exciting wine in the Finger Lakes region.

Steve has access to five separate Riesling vineyards, each of which presents its unique personality, giving him the opportunity to make use of Riesling's wonderful versatility—and, it's a grape variety that excels at a range of wine styles. We choose to produce two styles: dry and semi-dry.

Our Dry Riesling highlights the variety's austere yet bracing acidity—you might call it the variety's lemony side. Following its lemon-citrus aroma, the Dry Riesling delivers mouth-watering freshness and crispness accented by a mineral-like spine that runs through its center. Pair our Dry Riesling with various seafood dishes with mild sauces, butter over vegetables and mushrooms or fine fatty cheeses, and you can't go wrong.

WINE CELLAR STORIES

Riesling's original home is Germany, where the Romans made their most eastern outpost, and the waning empire's country estate for their waning emperors. The vines thrive in cool mountainous regions—which is exactly what makes Riesling the queen of the Finger Lakes.

Grilled Peach Salad with Truffled Raspberry Vinaigrette

Peaches take wonderfully to the grill, and their luscious sweetness marries perfectly with a bit of smoke. For this sophisticated summer salad, the peaches soften and caramelize over a moderate fire before being dressed with raspberry vinaigrette, local cheddar, and toasted walnuts.

Ingredients:

- 4 peaches, pitted and cut in quarters
- 12 ounces salad greens
- 1 cup toasted walnuts
- 4 ounces cheddar cheese, small dice
- 1/2 pint fresh raspberries
- 1/4 cup white wine vinegar
- 3/4 cup olive oil
- 1 tablespoon white truffle oil
- 1 teaspoon salt

Add raspberries, salt and vinegar to a blender. Blend together, then drizzle in oil slowly until incorporated. Reserve. Lightly oil and salt peaches, then grill two minutes on each side. Toss greens, and peaches with one ounce of vinaigrette. Top off with the toasted walnuts and cheese.

Makes four servings.

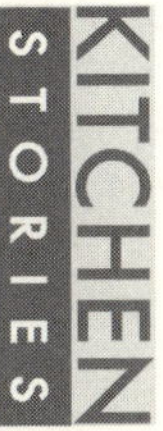

Our local source for aged "Deep Seneca" farmstead cheddar cheese is Sunset View Creamery in nearby Odessa, using milk from the farm's "closed herd" cows. Sunset View Farm has been in the Hoffman family since 1905.

Tuna Tartare with Citrus Salad and Wasabi Aioli

Dry Riesling proves a formidable match to the broad flavor range of fresh fruit, raw tuna, and wasabi. After savoring the taste of the tuna delicately dipped in its accoutrement, a sip of the wine accentuates each component, especially the wasabi and garlic, and with hints of refreshing citrus, the wine becomes a kindred companion to the fresh fruit.

Ingredients:

8 ounces yellow fin sashimi grade tuna, chopped fine
1/8 teaspoon sesame oil
1 teaspoon sea salt
2 grapefruit segments
2 lemon segments
2 lime segments
2 orange segments
2 teaspoon wasabi paste
1 cup mayonnaise
1 teaspoon garlic, minced and lightly toasted

In a mixing bowl, fold together tuna, sesame and sea salt. Reserve. In another bowl, mix all segments of fruit and set aside. In a third bowl, mix wasabi, mayo and garlic. Divide ingredients between four plates. Place the tuna in the center of plate. Arrange the citrus salad around the plate and serve with a dollop of the wasabi aioli.

Makes four servings.

The intriguing Japanese wasabi root has a fruity, vegetal fragrance and a spiciness that stimulates the palate with balanced heat, experienced more in the sinus than on the tongue.

Autumn Pasta with Andouille Sausage

Warm up an autumn evening with sautéed vegetables and coarse-grained, smoked andouille sausage anchoring this sumptuous supper dish. Dry Riesling is high in fresh, fruity acidity, tantalizing the appetite, counterbalancing the richness of the buttery cream sauce. With this mix of flavor profiles, you may be tempted to bring both a dry and semi-dry Riesling to the table, and then have fun exploring which version is a better match.

In a large sauté pan lightly brown butter, then add garlic and butternut squash; cook for three minutes. Add andouille and cook for four more minutes. Add kale, thyme, lemon juice and crème fraiche and cook for five minutes. Add hot fettuccini and toss together. Season with salt and pepper to taste.

Makes four servings.

Ingredients:

- 1 pound fettuccini pasta, cooked
- 8 ounces andouille sausage, diced
- 1 cup butternut squash, diced small
- 2 cups kale, chiffonade (thinly sliced)
- 1 tablespoon garlic, minced
- 1 lemon, juiced
- 1 tablespoon fresh thyme leaves
- 1/4 cup unsalted butter
- 2 cups crème fraiche

Evergreen Farm is our source for local kale. Cold improves its eating quality and its hardiness permits harvest after many other fresh vegetables have become unavailable.

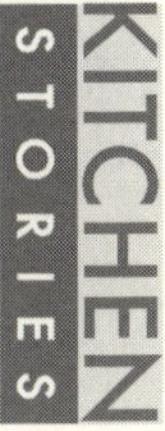

Mushroom, Spinach and Goat Cheese Ravioli with Pesto Cream Sauce

This dish is a symphony of flavor profiles and a showcase for some of our favorite local ingredients. Earthy shiitakes and bold wilted spinach seem fated to be together, and when matched with both goat cheese and cream sauce, Dry Riesling cuts through richness and complexity, preparing the palate for the next delicious bite. Each portion should include five raviolis.

Ingredients:

- 4 ounces shitake mushrooms, thinly sliced, stems removed
- 4 ounces spinach
- 2 ounces goat cheese
- 2 ounces olive oil
- 1 teaspoon salt
- 1/2 teaspoon black pepper, ground
- 1 package wonton wrap

For the pesto cream sauce:

- 4 ounces basil
- 1/4 cup toasted pine nuts
- 1/4 cup extra virgin olive oil
- 2 cloves garlic
- 2 teaspoons salt
- 1 teaspoon black pepper
- 1/4 cup parmesan cheese
- 2 cups heavy cream

To make the ravioli: add one ounce of olive oil to a sauté pan over medium-high heat. Sautee the mushrooms for about five minutes, until light brown and crisp. Set aside. Cook spinach with one ounce of olive oil for about three minutes or until wilted. Cool in refrigerator. Once ingredients are cool, add goat cheese, salt, pepper, mushrooms, and spinach, and mix well. Wet the wonton edges with water and place one teaspoon of mixture in the middle. Place another wonton on top and press around the edges. Once all raviolis are made, place six quarts of water to boil and cook for about four minutes. Serve with pesto cream sauce.

To make the pesto cream sauce: in a food processor add the pine nuts, garlic, salt, pepper, parmesan cheese, basil, and extra virgin olive oil. Pulse to an even consistency. Pour cream to a sauce pan over medium-high heat and reduce by one-third. Add one-quarter cup of the pesto, simmer for three minutes and serve over the pasta.

Makes six servings.

In the spirit of wine country cuisine, cheese made from goat milk has become a staple in Finger Lakes kitchens, mirroring the tradition of France's Loire Valley, home of both wine growing and countless herds of goats.

Pan-Seared Atlantic Halibut

The obvious match to this lovely springtime dish is well-chilled Dry Riesling, which picks up perfectly the layers of textures and flavors of the firm, flaky fish, fluffy, saffron-scented couscous, buttery vegetables, and creamy, garlicky sauce. The remarkably versatile wine harmonizes without overwhelming any of the components.

Ingredients:

4 8-ounce portions of halibut
2 tablespoons virgin olive oil
I cup vegetable stock
I cup couscous
I/4 teaspoon saffron
I tablespoon extra virgin olive oil
I/2 pound French beans
I tablespoon butter
I pint cherry tomatoes
To taste salt and pepper

For the sauce:

I cup peas
I teaspoon minced garlic
I teaspoon minced shallots
2 cups heavy cream
To taste salt and pepper

To make the couscous: in a small pot over medium-high heat, add vegetable stock, saffron, and extra virgin olive oil. Bring to a boil. Place the couscous in a mixing bowl. Add stock to couscous and cover bowl with plastic. Let sit for approximately ten minutes. Using a fork, fluff the couscous and season with salt and pepper.

To make the pea sauce: sweat the garlic and shallots in a small sauce pan for about three minutes, then add heavy cream and allow it come up to a simmer. Add the peas and simmer for two more minutes. Remove from the stove and puree in the blender. Season with salt and pepper.

To make the vegetables: wash the cherry tomatoes and cut length-wise. Clip off the stem ends of the French beans and wash. In a sauté pan, add butter and beans over medium-high heat and cook for approximately four minutes. Add the cherry tomatoes and cook for another two minutes. Season to taste with salt and pepper.

To make the halibut: heat a large sauté pan to medium-high heat, then add virgin olive oil. Place the halibut in the pan and sear for approximately four minutes, until the fish slightly browns and forms a crust.

Pour pea sauce at the bottom of each plate. Add couscous to the center and place the halibut on top. Arrange the vegetables around the fish.

Makes four servings.

Semi-Dry Riesling

In Germany, Riesling wines are labeled according to the sugar levels reached at harvest. Still, when it is finished and bottled, a certain style of German wine known as Auslese (owz-laiz-ay), usually falls within a mid range of sweetness, a range that we in America identify either as semi-dry (the bottom range of Auslese sweetness) or semi-sweet (the upper range of Auslese sweetness).

Our Semi-Dry Riesling has all the attributes of our Dry Riesling and then some. Its acidity is bracing, its sweetness is judicious, its body is full, and its finish is lengthy. It is also an extremely enticing wine, in large measure because of its powerful aromatics.

Peaches or apricot aromas identify our Semi-Dry Riesling. Sticking your nose in the glass replaces a walk in the orchard in spring. Fruit is the theme even as you taste the wine—like tropical fruit with a zing. Yet, the wine's structure—how it feels in your mouth—is so delicate and elegant it conjures the image of cumulus clouds.

Many find sipping a semi-dry wine its own pleasure. But you can extend that pleasure immeasurably when you pair our Semi-Dry Riesling with food. In the wine cellar, Steve creates the wine to emphasize its outstanding and intriguing balance between acid and sugar and its overall fruitiness and density; in the restaurant, Orlando challenges those attributes with creative concoctions like gingered or nut-infused fish, sweet and sour pork, hardy root vegetables, bitter greens, and poached fruits.

Semi-Dry Riesling is also the rare wine that can stand up to salads topped with vinegar-based dressing.

WINE CELLAR STORIES

In the wine industry, you often hear Riesling referred to as the Queen of white wines. The reference is not made to its femininity, although it could be, but to the wine's overall elegance, grace, and consistent beauty.

Essence of Beet Soup

Freshly-pulled, deep crimson beets are truly beautiful and delicious. The sweet, rich, earthy flavors of local "Red Ace" beets come alive in this very tasty beet soup that's so simple to make. The off-dry Riesling adds a splash of vibrancy and awesome aromatics. For added creaminess and a lovely presentation, we swirl this vibrantly colored soup with sour cream. Serve hot or chilled.

In a stock pot, simmer beets in the stock and vinegar for one hour. Strain through a paper coffee filter, then add the sugar, and wine. Season with salt and pepper as desired. Garnish with sour cream and some julienned beets.

Makes four servings.

Ingredients:

2 pounds raw beets peeled and chopped
40 ounces chicken stock
1 ounce red wine vinegar
1 tablespoon sugar
8 ounces Glenora Semi-Dry Riesling
2 teaspoon kosher salt
1/8 teaspoon ground white pepper

Don't discard the tops of your next bunch of beets. The dark-green leaves taste a lot like kale, Swiss chard, or even spinach, and they may be cooked or served fresh in salads.

Watermelon and Watercress Salad

This light, refreshing summer salad provides an extended palate experience. First, you taste the cool, sweet watermelon, then the vibrant, peppery watercress. Next is the tang and texture contrast of onions. The finesse and expressive flavors of the off-dry Riesling handles these different flavors quite nicely.

Ingredients:

2 bunches watercress
1 red onion, sliced very thin
1 ounce white wine vinegar
2 ounces olive oil
1/2 pound seedless watermelon, in melon ball scoops

Remove stems from the watercress. Wash and spin dry. Keep refrigerated until ready to use. For the dressing, place the vinegar in a bowl and whisk in the oil, and season with salt and pepper to taste. Toss the dressing with the onions, watercress and watermelon in a bowl, and serve.

Makes four servings.

A seedless watermelon is tasty if you select a ripe specimen, but they cannot replace old-fashioned watermelons with seeds for feeding the kids on the lawn.

Bulgur Salad with Green Onions

Bulgur is made by soaking and cooking the whole wheat kernel, drying it and then removing part of the bran and cracking the remaining kernel into small pieces. Its nutty character makes a great starting point for a salad loaded with texture and bursting with flavor. A touch of sweetness from the wine is perfect counterpoint to the tang of paprika.

Ingredients:

- 8 ounces bulgur grain, fine or medium
- 2 ounces olive oil
- 1 ounce white wine vinegar
- 1/2 ounce tomato paste
- 1 teaspoon sweet paprika
- 1/2 teaspoon hot paprika
- 5 ounces scallions, sliced
- 1-3/4 quarts water

Wash and rinse bulgur. In a medium sauce pan heat one ounce of the oil over medium-high heat. Add the scallions and sauté for about thirty seconds, then add the tomato paste. Reduce heat to medium and cook for one minute. Add the bulgur and stir until coated with the oil, then add the water and paprika. Bring to a boil on high heat and simmer for about twenty minutes or until all the water has been absorbed. Allow to sit for ten minutes, then add one ounce of oil and the vinegar, and mix well.

Makes four servings.

Making wheat into bulgur is an ancient process that originated in the Mediterranean region and has been an integral part of Middle Eastern cuisine for thousands of years.

Pan-Seared Trout with Toasted Almonds

Semi-Dry Riesling has a distinctive floral and apple-like aroma and mixes in mineral elements from its vineyard source. Adding a splash of wine to the pan intensifies and enhances the savory flavor of the fish, while the slight, nutty note in the wine finds a kindred spirit in the toasted almonds.

Dredge the trout in the flour and shake off the excess flour. Season with salt and pepper. Heat oil in a sauté pan over medium heat and sauté for three minutes on each side to a golden brown color. Set aside and keep warm. Wipe out pan and add butter. Cook to a light brown color, then add almonds and coat with butter. Add parsley, thyme, lemon juice, and Riesling. Simmer for three minutes and serve over the trout.

Makes four servings.

Ingredients:

4 6-ounce trout fillets
1 cup all purpose flour
2 ounces vegetable oil
5 ounces unsalted butter
2 ounces slivered almonds
2 ounces lemon juice
1 ounces chopped parsley
1 teaspoon fresh thyme leaves
1/2 ounce Glenora Semi-Dry Riesling
To taste salt
To taste ground black pepper

Trout figures more often in English poetry than any other fish. Lord Byron spoke of "trout not stale." And, according to Shakespeare, "Lie thou there; for here comes the trout that must be caught with tickling."

Ginger-Marinated Baked Salmon

Honey and ginger provide a sweet and spicy flavor bath, enhancing but not overpowering the rich flavor of the salmon. The residual sugar and natural acidity of Semi-Dry Riesling supports the meatiness and high oil content of the fish and provides contrast to the spicy tang of the ginger and saltiness of the soy sauce. An hour of marinating is all that is required; any longer and it will affect the texture of the salmon.

Ingredients:

- 2 pounds salmon fillet, pin bones removed
- 1/2 cup soy sauce
- 1 ounce ginger, sliced and peeled
- 1/4 cup honey
- 1 lime zest
- 4 garlic cloves thinly sliced
- 2 ounces vegetable oil

Mix the ginger, soy, honey, lime zest, garlic and vegetable oil. Place the salmon in a container; pour over the marinade and cool in refrigerator for about an hour. Place the salmon on a sheet pan and bake in a 400-degree oven for about ten minutes.

Makes four servings.

Ginger is mentioned in ancient Chinese, Indian and Middle Eastern writings, and has long been prized for its aromatic, culinary and medicinal properties.

Sautéed Pork Medallions with Sweet-and-Sour Sauce

A bit of sweetness in the Riesling allows many pleasurable combinations that can harmoniously connect to one another. The pork loin is a meaty, relatively tender cut with a large center eye, dense texture, and full-bodied flavor. In this dish, the wine's ripe fruit and balancing acidity provide a successful partnership with the pork and its coating of mouthwatering sweet and sour sauce, prepared with simple ingredients. To "sweat" the shallots, let them cook until tender, about five minutes or so.

Ingredients:

- 1-1/2 pounds pork loin cut in 1/4 inch slices
- 1 cup all purpose flour
- 1/4 cup vegetable oil
- To taste salt
- To taste ground black pepper

For the sweet & sour sauce:

- 1 tablespoon shallots, minced
- 1 ounce honey
- 1 ounce white wine vinegar
- 1 tablespoon lemon juice
- 1/8 teaspoon crushed red pepper
- 8 ounces chicken stock
- To taste salt
- To taste ground black pepper

Place oil to just cover the bottom of a sauté pan over medium-high heat. Season each slice of pork with salt and pepper, then lightly coat with the flour. Cook each piece to a golden brown color on each side (about two minutes). Once the pork is cooked, wipe out the pan with a paper towel and proceed to make the sauce.

Sweat shallots in the sauté pan. Add honey, vinegar, crushed red pepper, and lemon juice, and bring to a simmer. Add chicken stock and reduce to half. Season to taste. Serve over sautéed pork medallions.

Makes four servings.

The sweet and sour preparation of pork is a popular treat on Chinese New Year's Eve. Since the Cantonese word for sour sounds like the word for grandchildren, families believe that serving this dish will help ensure that they have more grandchildren in the New Year.

Baby Bok Choy

Humble in its presentation, the crisp texture and appealing flavor of baby bok choy is one of the pleasures of spring. While green vegetables can be hard to pair with wine, the almost bitter leaves and sweet, succulent stems of this intriguing vegetable offer an inspired pairing with Semi-Dry Riesling. It's a side dish that sings with flavor.

Ingredients:

6 baby bok choy
1 tablespoon unsalted butter
1 tablespoon shallots, minced
1/4 teaspoon garlic, minced
6 quarts water, boiling
To taste salt
To taste ground black pepper

Remove blemished leaves from the bok choy. Quarter and wash. Place in boiling water for about two to three minutes, until the bottom of the vegetable becomes tender. Remove from water and reserve. In a separate pan add the butter over medium heat. Once the butter is melted add shallots and garlic for about two minutes. Toss in the bok choy and season with salt and pepper.

Makes four servings.

KITCHEN STORIES

Shanghai, or baby bok choy is a miniature version of bok choy, more tender than the larger variety cultivated in China since ancient times. "Choy" is the word for a Chinese character that means "vegetable"; "bok" means white, referring to its white stems.

Riesling-Poached Peaches

Seneca Lake is home to some of the best peach orchards in the Northeast, and blossoming trees that can be seen from the roadside let us know when fruit season is under way. The buds that form in winter become the flowers in the spring that grow into the fruit of the summer. Poaching brings out a little "zip" in Red Haven, a local freestone, early-season variety, heightened by peach fruit sentiments in the off-dry Riesling.

Ingredients:

4 cups water
1 cups sugar
4 peaches
1 cup Glenora Semi-Dry Riesling
4 servings vanilla ice cream

Bring water, Riesling and sugar to a boil in a sauce pot. Add peaches and simmer for about thirty minutes. Remove peaches from the liquid and peel. Cut each peach in half and remove pits. Slice peaches and serve with vanilla ice cream.

Makes four servings.

KITCHEN STORIES

The easiest way to pit freestone peaches is to make a cut along the seam all the way around and through the fruit down to the pit. Then twist each half in opposite directions.

GEWURZTRAMINER

Gewurztraminer is probably the king of the aromatic grape varieties. As Steve says, "there's nothing like the aroma of Gewurztraminer fermenting."

This truly interesting grape variety is also a relative scalawag: if you wait a day too long before picking it, its acidity can fall lower than is comfortable for the wine's stability and lively taste, but if you pick too early, you won't gain all of its powerful aromatics.

Steve's always watchful eye is extra careful when overseeing Gewurztraminer's development in the Glenora Farms vineyard that he can see from his office window. He walks the vineyard in late September and early October, when the grapes are reaching their peak—he's looking for grapes when the aromatics are at peak and when pH and acidity are in perfect balance. The only way to do this is to randomly pick grapes from the vines and sample them. He must also make a trip to the other side of the lake, where more Gewurztraminer grows for him to select.

When they are ready on all sides of the lake, Steve makes sure that the grape picking is swift and the Gewurztraminer grapes rest in bins in the cool overnight, so that the brief skin contact allows the pulp to assimilate the grapes' aromatics fully and completely.

A whiff of Gewurztraminer is like standing in a rose garden on a clear day and breathing deeply. A taste of the wine is like a cross between pepper and ginger—some say it is like the oriental lychee nut. Gewurztraminer is definitely a wine for spicy food like sausages, and it excels as an accompaniment to wild game or as a foil for sweet/sour taste marriages.

WINE CELLAR STORIES

The Traminer grape was first identified in the Dolomite Mountains of Northeastern Italy. A member of the aromatic Muscat grape family, Gewurztraminer is just one of a few grapes in the Traminer variety. Its name in German means "Spicy-traminer."

Pear Salad with Peppered-Cider Vinaigrette

Grown in the Malabar region of southern India, Tellicherry black peppercorns are left on the vine long enough to develop deep fruity and floral notes. They add a whiff of incense and lingering warmth to the vinaigrette. Gewurztraminer provides an ideal foil to the complexity of flavors.

Ingredients:

- 12 ounces arugula
- 2 pears, sliced thin
- 1/4 cup toasted almond
- 1/2 cup parmesan cheese, shaved
- 1 shallot, sliced
- 5 Tellicherry black peppercorns
- 1 quart apple cider
- 1 tablespoon pasteurized egg yolk
- 1/2 cup apple cider vinegar
- 1 tablespoon mustard
- 1-1/4 cup vegetable oil

Place the shallots, black peppercorns and apple cider in a pot and reduce liquid to one-quarter. Place the mustard, vinegar, egg yolk and reduction in a blender and puree. Leave blender running and drizzle in the vegetable oil until fully incorporated. Mix arugula, sliced pears, toasted almond together with two ounces of the cider vinaigrette. Arrange on plates and serve with the shaved parmesan cheese on top.

Makes four servings.

Our apple cider is sourced from Red Jacket Orchards in nearby Geneva. Red Jacket presses all year round, so we get fresh cider any time of year.

"Gewurz-Steamed" Littleneck Clams

Steamed in a hearty Gewurztraminer broth, intensified with the heat of chili black bean sauce and smoky flavor of bacon, clams retain their strong, rich taste. Synergy between a dish of food and a glass of wine happens when the same wine is added to both—an accompanying chilled, spicy Gewurztraminer takes the edge off the salt and cleanses the palate. If desired, serve with a small cup of melted butter for dipping clams along with a fresh loaf of warm, crusty bread.

Ingredients:

4 cloves garlic, thinly sliced
1/4 pound bacon lardons
1/2 cup Glenora Gewurztraminer
48 Littleneck clams
2 teaspoons chili black bean sauce
4 scallions, sliced thin

In a large stock pot over medium heat, render bacon for ten minutes, then add the garlic and cook for one minute. Wash clams in cold water, and discard any clams that are partially opened. Add the clams and wine and cover for four minutes or until clams open. Shake the pot periodically to be sure that the clams are heated and steamed evenly. Add chili sauce and scallions and toss together. Divide the ingredients evenly into shallow soup plates.

Makes four servings.

KITCHEN STORIES

Lardons are small pieces of thick cut bacon, sold ready-chopped. As an alternative to lardons, thick rashers of bacon can be cut lengthwise into strips and diced into small pieces.

Chipotle-Marinated Chicken Sandwich

The marinade owes its not-so-subtle flavors to smoky chipotle (say chee-poht-lay) peppers, pungent garlic, and tart, tangy lime juice. An overnight bath in the spicy marinade helps transform one-dimensional chicken into an extraordinary meal. What's needed alongside is a rich, spicy Gewurztraminer for balance.

Ingredients:

4 chicken breasts, 4 ounces each
1-1/2 tablespoon chipotle peppers
1 tablespoon cilantro
1 clove garlic
1 lime, juiced
1/4 cup oil
4 Kaiser rolls
1 bunch leaf lettuce
2 tomatoes, sliced
1 small red onion, grilled
1 cup mayonnaise

For the marinade, place in a blender and puree chipotle, cilantro, garlic, lime juice and oil. Clean any excess fat off the chicken and place in the marinade for twenty-four hours. Grill the chicken and toast the Kaiser rolls. For the mayonnaise, place one-half tablespoon of the chipotle pureed with the mayonnaise. Spread mayonnaise on the bread and build the sandwiches with lettuce, tomatoes, onion and grilled chicken.

Makes four servings.

The chipotle or "ahumado" process consists in placing jalapeno peppers on wood or metal grills inside a smoking chamber that receives the smoke from a natural wood fire.

Spanish-Style Penne with Chorizo Sausage

The robust flavors and warm spices of chorizo tickle the taste buds and give this dish the feel of Spanish cooking. Fava beans temper a bit of the sausage's heat, yet there is nothing subtle about this deeply-flavored dish. Luckily, the spicy richness of Gewurztraminer can handle it.

Ingredients:

1 pound penne pasta, cooked
1 pound chorizo, sliced one-quarter inch thick
2 tablespoons olive oil
2 tablespoons red curry paste
4 cups heavy cream
2 tablespoons cilantro
2 tablespoons garlic, thinly sliced
1/2 cup fava beans

In a large skillet, add the oil and cook garlic over medium heat for one minute. Cook chorizo for two minutes, then add the heavy cream and red curry paste. Continue cooking until reduced by half. Add pasta, cilantro and fava beans.

Makes four servings.

Bright, citrusy cilantro is the secret ingredient in this dish, bringing out the flavors of the other ingredients, never masking or overpowering them.

Fried Shrimp with Asian Dipping Sauce

Dishes with bold, spicy flavors share a natural flavor affinity with bold, spicy wines. The inherent spiciness of Gewurztraminer is unmistakable and a charming compliment to the strong flavors of this Asian-inspired dish. Break out the chopsticks and the corkscrew.

Mix together the egg, water and flour for the batter. Dip the shrimp in the batter and fry in 350-degree oil for about five minutes, then place on a paper towel to absorb any excess oil.

To make the dipping sauce: mix together the soy sauce, white wine vinegar, water, garlic, green onion, ginger, dry mustard, hot bean paste and honey. Place in refrigerator until ready to use.

Makes four servings.

Ingredients:

16-16/20 shrimp, peeled, deveined (tail on)
1 egg
5 ounces water
1 cup all purpose flour

For the dipping sauce:

2 ounces soy sauce
1 ounce white wine vinegar
1 ounce water
1 garlic, minced
1 green onion, minced
1/4 teaspoon ginger minced
1/4 teaspoon dry mustard
1/4 teaspoon hot bean paste
1 tablespoon honey

KITCHEN STORIES

History shows that as far back as the seventh century, Marco Polo commented on the abundance of shrimp in East Asian (Chinese) marketplaces.

PINOT BLANC

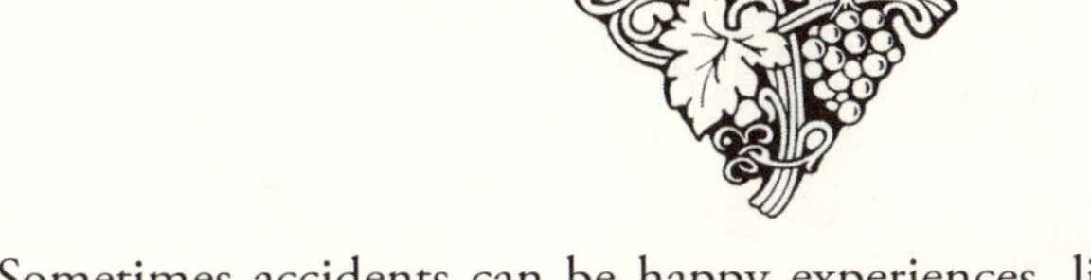

Sometimes accidents can be happy experiences, like the one concerning Glenora Wine Cellars and Pinot Blanc—it's a kind of detective story.

In the late 1980s, while visiting the Finger Lakes region, during a walk through Jim Hazlitt's vineyards, an ampelographer (a person who identifies or classifies grapevine varieties) noticed that what everyone thought were Chardonnay vines were in fact Pinot Blanc, maybe the only Pinot Blanc in the region at the time. Except for a leaf variation, the vines look similar to each other.

Hazlitt was then and remains today one of the important grape growers in the region who supply Glenora Wine Cellars. His vineyards are located on the east shores of Seneca Lake, in that area known locally as "the banana belt," for its relatively warmer microclimate.

Never ceasing to seize an opportunity, we immediately began to produce Pinot Blanc varietal wine, and Steve has perfected work with the variety over the years. He watches carefully over all grape varieties, but he is extra careful with Pinot Blanc. Like its aromatic cousins, Pinot Blanc is extremely sensitive to its short ripening window. Because it is so sensitive, this is one variety that truly reflects each unique vintage season.

It is considered an aromatic variety yet the style of wine Steve strives for is bracing and austere. He tempers the wine by fermenting it in older barrels and then aging it in the same, so as not to give it the flavors of oak, but to give it a rounder, viscous mouth feel, along with an earthy, vanilla-like aroma.

Still, the Pinot Blanc comes with crispness to cut through the oils of big fishes, plus depth that makes it easy to pair with classic veal and other meat dishes topped with a French-style creamy sauce. Vegetables under hollandaise wouldn't be a bad idea either. Additionally, this is a perfect wine for that opening canapé or cheese course.

WINE CELLAR STORIES

Like its red relative, Pinot Noir, the Blanc version is a fickle producer. It presents a short picking window during ripening season, and because of its tight pinecone-like clusters (hence, the name Pinot), over-ripening can quickly spread throughout the grapes.

Ultimate Grilled Cheese Sandwich

In a recipe that elevates the humble grilled cheese sandwich to an art form, this gooey, sinfully delicious version is made with cheddar cheese melted between slices of crispy sourdough bread, with heirloom tomatoes and fresh basil. The secret to this sandwich is cooking over low heat, which brings out subtle smokey flavors in the cheese, counterpoint to a wine that's easy to quaff.

Ingredients:

- 8 slices sourdough bread
- 8 ounces cheddar cheese, sliced
- 2 large heirloom tomatoes, sliced 1/4-inch thick
- 16 fresh basil leaves
- 8 tablespoons unsalted butter

In a large sauté pan on medium heat, add two tablespoons of butter and place one slice of bread. Add two slices of cheese, two leaves of basil, and two slices of tomato. Add basil, cheese and bread to finish the top half. Once one side has become light golden brown, flip the bread to the other side and let brown.

Makes four servings.

Aged, sharp New York cheddar cheese has a hearty flavor, perfect as the centerpiece of a childhood favorite we never seem to outgrow.

Farmhouse Cheeses

Bite-size nibbles of cheese can be a wonderful way to subdue dinner party appetites while the host prepares the meal. Keep the selection light in both flavor and richness. Some favorite local cheese pairings with Pinot Blanc include a soft, moist, un-aged goat cheese from Lively Run, a gouda/muenster cross named "Red Meck" from Finger Lakes Farmstead Cheese, and a mild cheddar from Sunset View Creamery.

Ingredients:

8 ounces fresh goat cheese
8 ounces gouda or muenster
8 ounces mild cheddar
Wine crackers

Form the goat cheese into marble-size balls. Cut the other cheese into small, bite-size pieces. Arrange on a platter with some fresh grapes and wine crackers.

Makes four servings.

The important thing to remember is not to fill guests up too much. When serving a selection of cheese before dinner, choose no more than two or three different varieties.

Chilled Cucumber-Dill Soup with Grilled Shrimp

This delicious soup is a cool, smooth, refresher, perfect for summertime entertaining, especially when framed with the bright fruit of Pinot Blanc. For an elegant and unique presentation, serve this soup in chilled cocktail glasses, with shrimp as a garnish.

Cook onions and celery in butter until onions are translucent. Add the cucumber and chicken stock to pot and simmer for about thirty minutes. Puree in a blender and strain. Add sour cream and heavy cream and one-quarter bunch of chopped dill. Season with salt, pepper, lemon juice and tabasco. Serve chilled with shrimp and dill sprigs.

Makes four servings.

Ingredients:

12 shrimp, large, grilled, sliced in half lengthwise
1/2 pound Spanish onion, diced
1/2 pound celery, diced
16 ounces chicken stock
1 ounce butter
3 pounds cucumber, peeled, sliced and diced
12 ounces sour cream
4 ounces heavy cream
1/2 bunch dill
1 tablespoon kosher salt
1/2 teaspoon white pepper
Tabasco sauce, to taste
3 ounces lemon juice

At the tail end of summer, our local Finger Lakes farmer's markets are bursting with fresh English cucumbers, prized for thin skin and minimal seeds.

Chantenay Carrot and Fennel Salad

A local farmer supplies our kitchen with Chantenay carrots, a crisp variety with gorgeous bright-orange flesh and a sweet flavor that finds a bracing comrade in fresh aromatic fennel. The fleeting anise flavor is buoyed by a tangy mustard vinaigrette in a bright and playful yet beautifully wine-friendly dish.

Ingredients:

2 ounces blanched almonds
2 Chantenay carrots, sliced thin
1 fennel bulb, shaved thin
2 endives
1/2 cup fresh peas
2 tablespoons sherry vinegar
6 tablespoons extra-virgin olive oil
1/2 teaspoon Dijon mustard

Lightly toast the almonds in a pan to a golden brown color. With a peeler make thin slices of carrots and fennel, then place in a water bath with ice. Pull apart the leaves from the endive and place in a bowl with the peas. Add in the carrots and fennel after taking out of the water and drying them well. In separate bowl add in the mustard and vinegar and whisk in the virgin olive oil. Toss vegetables with the dressing.

Makes four servings.

KITCHEN STORIES

As the name suggests, the Chantenay carrot originated from the Chantenay region of France. Early references to the Chantenay carrot can be found back in the mid-1800s, when it was used in medicine.

Pan-Seared Striped Bass

Wild striped bass swims the waters along the East Coast. Moderately fatty, wild bass has a juicy, sweet flavor, and a large flake with a firm, steak-like texture. Deft pan searing will provide a delicious crispy skin—one of the best things about striped bass. A wine's acidity can bring out the essence of an ingredient, so the marriage of bass and Pinot Blanc is a happy one.

Ingredients:

1-1/2 pounds striped bass, divided into 6-ounce portions
2 tablespoons olive oil
To taste salt
To taste black pepper
2 tablespoons unsalted butter
1 ounce Glenora Pinot Blanc
2 tablespoons fresh parley, chopped

Add olive oil to a skillet over medium-high heat. Place the fish skin side down for four minutes or until skin is crisp. Turn and cook for three more minutes on the other side. Remove the fish from the pan, add butter, then deglaze with white wine. Season to taste with salt and pepper.

Makes four servings.

The striped bass has been prized in America since colonial times. In 1670, Plymouth Colony established a free school with the income from coastal striped bass fisheries.

Pickled Vegetables

The vegetables have a nice crunch and are fun to eat. It's not a classic pairing, but the refreshingly aggressive profile in Pinot Blanc creates a provocative composition with the integrated flavors of this dish that sends taste buds though a sensory metamorphosis.

Ingredients:

- 1 cucumber, halved, seeded and sliced thin
- 1/2 cup rice wine vinegar
- 1 teaspoon granulated sugar
- 1 small carrot, thin julienne
- 1/2 daikon radish, thin julienne
- 1 orange, juiced
- 1 teaspoon salt

Simmer vinegar, orange juice and sugar over medium heat for five minutes. Let cool, then mix in remainder of ingredients and let set for about an hour before serving.

Makes four servings.

The sensual white daikon is a large Asian radish with a mild and sweet fresh flavor. Some exceptional daikons are as fat as footballs. Choose those that are firm and unwrinkled.

Spiked Butterscotch Pudding

Similarity of flavors between wine and food makes for pleasant combinations. The butter and butterscotch bouquet imparted by barrel fermentation not only enhances the Pinot Blanc fruit, it suggests pairing with a dessert from the childhood land of comfort food.

Ingredients:

2-1/4 cup milk
1 cup heavy cream
1 cup brown sugar
4 egg yolks
1/4 cup cornstarch
1 ounce milk
1/2 teaspoon vanilla extract
1 ounce scotch whiskey
1/2 teaspoon salt
3 ounces butter, unsalted

Step 1: in a sauce pan add milk, heavy cream and brown sugar, and bring to a simmer.

Step 2: in a separate bowl, add two ounces of the hot liquid to the egg yolks and mix, then add remainder of egg mixture in with the step one hot milk and cream mixture.

Step 3: mix together cornstarch and milk. Add to the mixture of steps one and two, along with vanilla, whiskey and salt.

Step 4: return mixture to the burner over medium-high heat and whisk until mixture comes to a boil and thickens.

Step 5: remove from heat and whisk in the butter. Spoon the pudding into 4-ounce ramekins and refrigerate.

Makes four servings.

The "scotch" portion of the term is a corruption of "scorch," in reference to the caramel or "burnt sugar" flavor and appearance, not to Scotch whiskey. But the flavors marry so well that we can't resist adding a little shot.

SIGNATURE SERIES

The Meritage Association (see page 117) sanctions both red and white wines, but like the reds, the whites must be produced only from grapes that are grown in the French Bordeaux region. We don't grow Bordeaux white varieties (Sauvignon Blanc, Semillion, and four others) so we created our own white wine blend produced solely from European grape varieties and we call that our Signature Series wine.

The Signature Series is produced from Pinot Blanc, Chardonnay, and Riesling. It is also an annual surprise. Since the three varieties have unique maturing time schedules, Steve is presented each year with one of a multiple of combinations of maturation. It's his job to pick out which combination will continue the consistent level of quality that he seeks.

The Signature Series blend changes each year to make full use of the results of each vintage.

Still, after a few vintages working with the white blend, Steve notices that the Pinot Blanc generally dominates the aroma. Since this is an aromatic variety, we view it as a good thing. There's 'vanilla and spice and everything nice' in that aroma.

In the taste, the Chardonnay lends breadth and depth to the feel of the wine and the Riesling provides a mineral-like spine and a resin-like feel on the tongue. Its clean, snappy, refreshing finish gives the Signature Series brightness and vibrancy.

While the style of Signature Series wines plays off each separate vintage, the wine's overall character remains a cross between French and German—did we say Alsatian? That's the area along the Rhine River that is itself a blend of France and Germany.

Consider sipping our Signature Series whites alongside foods with spice and power.

WINE CELLAR STORIES

The art of blending wine is as old as commercial wine itself. Blending is done for two reasons: sometimes, a combination of wines offers its unique and interesting qualities, and sometimes the vintage dictates that a blend will be better than a single-variety wine.

Chicken and Wild Rice Soup

Garlic and a splash of the Signature Series white wine give this chicken and rice soup an appealing flavor intensity. It's a wine country twist on an old-fashioned chicken and rice soup that we like to serve in the autumn. The wild rice adds an earthy, nutty flavor that pairs nicely with the full-bodied wine.

In a stock pot, add the olive oil and sweat the garlic and onions together for five minutes. Add the carrots, chicken, bay leaf, and thyme, and cook for another five minutes. Deglaze the pan with the wine. Add the lemon juice and celery and cook for five minutes, then add the chicken stock. After simmering for thirty minutes, add the cooked rice.

Makes four servings.

Ingredients:

1-1/2 quart chicken stock
1/2 cup wild rice, cooked
1 6-ounce chicken breast, small dice
1 bay leaf
1/2 teaspoon garlic minced
1/2 teaspoon dry thyme
1/2 onion, small dice
1 stick celery, small dice
2 carrots, small dice
1/2 cup Glenora Signature Series wine
1 tablespoon lemon juice
1 tablespoon olive oil

Native Americans harvested wild rice by paddling their canoes through the rice stalks growing naturally in lakes and rivers, gently tapping the heads with sticks to knock the mature seeds into the bottom of the boat.

Seared Salmon with Black Olive Relish and Charred-Tomato Coulis

The pronounced, buttery and rich flavor of salmon calls for a full bodied wine, and the Signature Series white blend is happy to oblige. Pan-searing locks in the fish's juicy flavor, but take care not to overcook. When the fish is done, it should show traces of bright orange when you peek inside with the tip of a paring knife. If the center color is a dull orange, the fish is overcooked.

Ingredients:

- 4 6-ounce wild salmon slices, skin on
- 4 vine ripe tomatoes, large
- 6 kalamata olives, pitted and quartered
- 1 tablespoon shallots, minced
- 1 teaspoon garlic, minced
- 1 teaspoon fresh thyme leaves
- 1-1/2 tablespoons red wine vinegar
- 1 tablespoon olive oil
- 1/4 cup vegetable oil
- 1 teaspoon salt
- 1/2 teaspoon black pepper

Pre-heat oven to 400 degrees. Season salmon with salt and pepper and set aside.

Char two of the tomatoes on the grill until the outer skin is black and starts to blister. Peel the outer skin off and place tomatoes in a blender. Add the salt and pepper and puree. Drizzle in the vegetable oil until fully incorporated, then reserve the coulis.

For the relish, deseed and small dice the remaining two tomatoes. In a mixing bowl, add the black olives, garlic, shallots, thyme, red wine vinegar, olive oil, diced tomatoes and a pinch of salt. Toss together and reserve.

For the salmon, in a large skillet over a medium-high heat, place two tablespoons of virgin olive oil. Add salmon and sear, skin side down, for about four minutes, then place in pre-heated oven for five minutes. On the bottom of each plate, pour a pool of the sauce, then place the salmon, skin side up, with black olive relish on top.

Makes four servings.

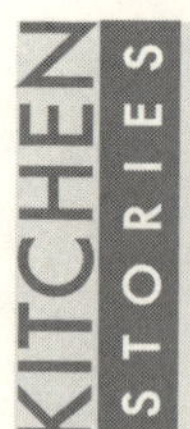

Perfect pan-searing depends on a very hot pan. Use a heavy cast-iron skillet, which heats evenly. Warm the pan before adding the oil to allow the pan to get hot without burning the oil.

Slow-Roasted Goose with Jicama Strawberry Salsa

In the fall, when fresh young geese come onto the market, we serve this dish with a delightful salsa on the side. Since all the meat on a goose is moist, dark, and flavorful, the full-bodied Signature Series blend provides an artful pairing. Slow roasting at low temperature drains the fat and tenderizes the meat.

Ingredients:

1 goose, approximately 10 pounds
6 thyme, sprigs
6 rosemary sprigs
6 garlic cloves
1 small jicama, peeled and small diced
6 strawberries, small diced
1 jalapeno, seeded and minced
2 tablespoon cilantro, chopped
2 limes, juiced

Pre-heat oven to 250 degrees. Remove necks and gizzards from the bird. Cut off the wing bone and trim excess fat and skin. Season the outside and inner cavity of the goose with salt and pepper. Inside the cavity place the garlic, thyme and rosemary. Place the goose in a hotel pan with a wire rack underneath to catch the drippings. Place in the oven for three hours, and every hour dump the excess drippings. For the salsa, place the jicama, strawberries, jalapeno, cilantro, and lime juice in a bowl and mix together with a pinch of salt. Carve the goose and serve with the salsa.

Makes four servings.

Jicama (pronounced HEE-ca-ma), called the "Mexican potato," is a large root vegetable with a thin brown skin and a white crunchy flesh. Its slightly sweet, nutty flavor lies between an apple and a water chestnut.

Seared Shredded Beef with Peppers and Onions

The depth and complexity of the Signature Series blend, developed by oak aging, proves there are actually times when white wine pairs successfully with beef. Naturally lean flank steak is one of the easiest cuts to shred by hand since the muscle is made up of long stringy fibers. The divine combination of sweet red peppers and sweet Spanish onions adds excitement to the dish.

Ingredients:

- 1 pound flank steak, cut into 8 pieces
- 1 red pepper, seeded and sliced
- 1-1/2 Spanish onions, thinly sliced
- 1 bay leaf
- 2 clove garlic, minced
- 1/4 cup lime juice
- 2 tablespoons olive oil
- 1 tablespoon salt
- 1 teaspoon ground black pepper
- 3 cups beef stock

In a large saucier pan, combine the beef stock, flank steak, red pepper, bay leaf and onion and bring to a boil. Let simmer for thirty minutes. Remove the flank steak and let cool. Using your hands, shred the beef by pulling apart the fibers. Strain the liquid and reserve with the peppers and onions. Add oil to the pan and cook the garlic for one minute. Add the onions and peppers, then add the shredded beef and lime juice. Stir together for two minutes. Add the stock, salt and pepper and cook until almost dry.

Makes four servings.

In Mexican cuisine, strips of flank steak, known as arrachera, are used to fill tortillas.

Oven-Roasted Fresh Ham with Honey Glaze

Roasted bone-in fresh ham is a Glenora Easter tradition, basted with a glaze that combines the sweetness of honey with the contrasting flavor of vinegar. The sugars in the glaze caramelize while baking, providing a glistening sheen, but because of the long cooking time, baste the glaze toward the end so it doesn't burn. The versatile Signature Series blend has enough power to complement this flavorful roast.

Ingredients:

- 12 pounds fresh ham; cut outer skin into diamond cuts
- 1 pound brown sugar
- 1/4 cup kosher salt
- 1 cup red wine vinegar
- 1 tablespoon salt
- 8 ounces honey
- 4 ounces chicken stock

Mix the brown sugar and salt together, then pack around the outside of the ham and let marinate overnight in the refrigerator. Pre-heat oven to 325 degrees. Remove ham from refrigerator and rub off excess sugar mixture and place in a roasting pan with a rack. Cook for four hours. Remove ham from the oven and transfer to a cutting board. Cover the ham loosely with foil and let rest for thirty minutes. Discard excess oil and place the roasting pan on stove top. Add the vinegar, salt, honey, and stock and let simmer for five minutes.

To carve the ham, start at the thick end and cut into thin slices, working against the grain. Pour honey glaze over ham slices and serve.

Makes ten servings.

Ham is the traditional centerpiece for Easter, a tradition that dates to pre-Christian Europe, when the pig was considered a symbol of luck.

Niagara

The Finger Lakes wine industry was built on local grapes, as opposed to grapes from other continents. You can still find many wines in the region that are produced from the old varieties of the Northeastern United States, and we offer one of them ourselves.

They may be local, but Niagara grapevines are like any other: they require careful attention and a response to their special needs. In the vineyard, Niagara grapes get better with age. That's why we blend out Niagara wine from three to four select decades-old vineyards. But care doesn't stop there.

In fact, the special care of Niagara extends right up to harvest, when this early to mid-September ripening variety gives us only hours to make our harvesting decision. We have to be ready when the grapes are ready—no hesitation—because Niagara is both an aromatic white grape variety and one that offers lower acidity. Balancing those two traits is paramount.

You might say that harvest begins in the Finger Lakes when you can smell Niagara. As the Niagara vineyards mature, their powerful aromatics are like a call to the wild, and we mean the real wild. Ripening Niagara grapes may in fact be nature's way of putting turkey and deer on notice that something good is about to happen to their diet.

Fragrant and fruity, almost like eating grapes from the vine, Niagara is a fine companion to light, picnic-like fare, cheese, fruits, and nuts.

Look closely at the following recipes and you'll see a nut based cookie favored by our own Gene Pierce, who, contrary to company rumor, does not eat peanut butter and drink Niagara on the job.

WINE CELLAR STORIES

Niagara is a hybrid developed in1868 by C.L. Hoag and B.W. Clark, from Niagara County, N.Y., when they crossed the Concord grape with the white Cassady grape. Commercial Niagara grapes hit the market in 1882 as table grapes and for juice.

Balsamic Glazed Chicken Wings

Adults experience a childlike pleasure in eating with their fingers, especially when there is a rich, sweet/tart balsamic sauce to lick off. A bottle of chilled Niagara is all you need to round out a perfect patio picnic.

Fry chicken wings in a fryer at 350 degrees for eight to ten minutes. In a separate pan, add balsamic vinegar, sugar, salt, pepper, and shallots and reduce over a medium-high heat for five to six minutes to a syrupy consistency. Add the butter, two tablespoon at a time, stirring constantly until butter is fully incorporated. In a mixing bowl, place the chicken wings and toss with balsamic glaze just before serving.

Makes four servings.

Ingredients:

12 chicken wings
2 cups balsamic vinegar
2 tablespoons minced shallots
6 tablespoons sugar
1/2 teaspoon salt
1/4 teaspoon ground black pepper
6 tablespoons unsalted butter

KITCHEN STORIES

Chicken wings became part of American culture thanks to "Mother" Teressa Bellisimo of the Anchor Bar in Buffalo, New York, who first created spicy chicken wings in 1964 as late-night bar food.

Cold Boiled Lobster with a Spiced Tomato Coulis

For a successful pairing, both the food and the wine should be made better and more interesting. When boiled lobster, enhanced with a spicy sauce, is paired with Niagara, both partners benefit from the mutual richness. Take care not to overcook lobsters—the tender meat will become tough and stringy.

Ingredients:
- 4 lobsters, 1 pound live
- 3 tomatoes, large
- 1 teaspoon Tabasco sauce
- 1 tablespoon lemon juice
- 2 tablespoon horseradish, grated fresh
- 2 teaspoon kosher salt
- 2 tablespoon olive oil
- 1 bunch chervil

Boil the lobsters in salted boiling water for twelve minutes. Remove from water and let cool in refrigerator. Blanch the tomatoes and remove outer skins. Place in a blender. Add the Tabasco, lemon juice, horseradish, and salt. Blend together for three minutes, then add in olive oil. Strain and reserve the coulis in the refrigerator. Remove the meat from the claw of the lobster. Cut lobster tails in half lengthwise with a large heavy knife. Place a pool of the coulis on the bottom of each plate. Form a circle with the lobster tail and arrange the claws in the center. Garnish each serving with a plush of chervil.

Makes four servings.

Live lobsters can be stored in the refrigerator for several hours by placing them in a large container covered with damp newspaper or seaweed. Including a piece of seaweed in the cooking pot adds a nice briny flavor.

Chocolate-Peanut Butter Cookies

A picnic basket wouldn't be complete without cookies. The sweet and salty combination of chocolate and peanut butter makes the perfect ending to an outing, and will hold up well in your picnic basket for hours. We have an ongoing debate about whether smooth or crunchy peanut butter make the best cookies. Women seem to favor smooth, while most men prefer crunchy.

Ingredients:

- 1-1/2 cups all purpose flour, sifted
- 1 tablespoon milk
- 1/2 cup white sugar
- 1/2 teaspoon baking soda
- 1/4 cup light corn syrup
- 1/4 teaspoon salt
- 1/2 cup shortening
- 1 cup peanut butter
- 1 cup semi-sweet chocolate chips

Combine flour, sugar, soda, and salt. Cut in shortening and peanut butter until mixture resembles coarse meal. Blend in syrup and milk. Shape into rolls two inches in diameter; chill. Slice one-eighth to one-quarter inch thick. Place half of the cookie slices on an ungreased cookie sheet; spread each with a half-teaspoon of peanut butter. Sprinkle chocolate chips on top of peanut butter. Cover with remaining cookies slices; seal edges with a flat fork. Bake at 350 degrees for twelve minutes, or until golden brown.

Makes forty-eight cookies.

KITCHEN STORIES

Peanut butter didn't become an ingredient in America's cookies until a recipe appeared in the 1931 edition of "Pillsbury's Balanced Recipes."

Red Wines and Recipes

Cabernet Sauvignon

When you think of tender European-style wine grapes, none beat the tenderness of Cabernet Sauvignon when grown in the Finger Lakes. That's why it takes a special vineyard site in this special region to grow the grapes for this special wine.

Scott Welliver's vineyard site is called Mason Road, a Seneca Lake location further south than his other vineyards and also closer to the lake, along steep slopes. This eastern shore location provides the Cabernet Sauvignon vineyard with a full dose of daily sun and the heat that comes with it.

They ripen in October, but before that time comes, Steve and his crew is out there cluster thinning to make sure that only the ripest grapes make it to the crusher. But he also lets some sections develop as they are, to provide him with two levels of ripeness just in case the vintage takes a turn for the worse when harvest approaches.

At the fermenter, Steve seeks an even 88 degrees F. temperature to draw out and stabilize color, and to cool things down when they get too hot, he performs what is known as the pump over—drawing juice from the bottom of the tank and pumping it into the top of the tank. Pumping over both cools and circulates the active yeast to keep the fermentation alive to its natural end.

The result, after careful oak aging, is a Cabernet Sauvignon wine with delicate depth and mouth feel plus an uncommon (for cool climate red wine), full structure. Close your eyes and you can imagine dark fruits like currents—

concentrate on your tongue and you can feel the wine's tannic backbone.

You can't go wrong with a hearty red meat dish to pair with Glenora's Cabernet Sauvignon, but you would also do well to consider rich mushroom dishes and roasted or grilled vegetables, not to mention a fine cheddar—oh well, we mentioned it anyway!

WINE CELLAR STORIES

Through the science of DNA, we now know that Cabernet Sauvignon's parents are the Cabernet Franc and Sauvignon Blanc vines. Imagine that: giving the child the two first names of its parents.

Poached Chayote Salad with Red Wine Vinaigrette

Beloved and cherished in Mexican, South American, and Caribbean cuisines, chayote squash is equally good in Finger Lakes cuisine. With a taste that suggests the combination of potato and cucumber, we partner chayote with local beets, onions, goat cheese, and (with a bit of whimsy) fresh dates. The complexity of flavors and intriguing textures compliment robust, assertive Cabernet Sauvignon.

Ingredients:

- 2 chayote squash
- 2 roasted large red beets
- 1 red onion, thinly sliced
- 1/2 cup red wine vinegar
- 1/4 cup olive oil
- 8 dates, sliced length wise
- 4 ounces goat cheese
- 1 tablespoon + 1 tablespoon salt
- 1/2 tablespoon pepper

Cut chayote into quarters and remove seeds. Place in a pot and cover with water. Add one tablespoon salt and simmer for fifteen minutes. Set aside. Cook beets in 375-degree oven for ninety minutes. Peel beets and dice into large chunks. For the vinaigrette, place the red wine vinegar in a bowl and whisk in the olive oil. Add one teaspoon of salt and a half-tablespoon of pepper. Cut chayote into thin slices and fan in center of plate. Toss the beets and dates together in two tablespoons of the vinaigrette and place around the chayote. Crumble the goat cheese on top. Place a few of the red onion slices around the plate and drizzle vinaigrette over the chayote and onions.

Makes four servings.

Chayote was cultivated by the ancient Aztecs and Mayans of Central America and over the centuries has been known by names like xuxu, sousous, chocho, one-seeded cucumber, pear squash, custard marrow, alligator pear, vegetable pear, and christophine.

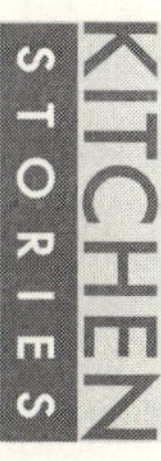

Savory Beef Empanadas

Empanadas literally mean "to cover in bread," and this Latin "street food" is traditionally made with whatever is at hand: meat, poultry, vegetables, cheese, fish, or sweet combinations. The tannic nature of Cabernet Sauvignon provides a reliable partner for these spicy, half-moon-shaped, beef-stuffed pies, meant to be devoured with gusto as a snack or a main dish.

Ingredients:

For the filling:
1 teaspoon olive oil
6 ounces ground beef
1 teaspoon chili powder
1/2 teaspoon cumin
1/4 teaspoon coriander
1 clove garlic, minced
1 teaspoon salt
1 teaspoon capers
1 teaspoon lime juice
2 tablespoon onion

For the dough:
3-1/4 ounce all purpose flour
1-1/2 teaspoon baking powder
2 ounces masa harina
1/2 teaspoon salt
2 ounces melted butter
3 ounces water
1 egg

Place oil and garlic in a saute pan and lightly toast until the garlic aroma is strong. Add onion and cook for an additional ten minutes. Add the ground beef and remaining ingredients. Cook until there is no pink in the meat. Place in refrigerator until ready to assemble empanada.

Mix together flour, baking powder, masa harina, and salt in a mixing bowl. Add butter and mix together. Add the egg and water gradually and mix together. Once the dough is formed, knead for about three to four minutes, then allow it to set for about fifteen minutes.

To assemble the empanadas, roll the dough a sixteenth of an inch thick and cut with a three-inch round cutter into twelve circles. Place three-quarters of a tablespoon of the filling in the center of dough. Rub the edge of the dough with water and fold the dough together and seal seams. Fry in a fryer set at 350 degrees for about two to three minutes on each side. Place on a paper towel to absorb excess oil, and serve hot.

Makes six servings.

Cabernet-Braised Short Ribs

For tender, succulent short ribs, one of the traditional methods of cooking is braising—searing the meat and simmering slowly, never rushed. Braising transforms the tough, rugged texture of short ribs to fork-cut tenderness, and deglazing with Cabernet Sauvignon enhances flavor while creating a bridge to the bottle of wine you'll be opening for dinner. Serve this satisfying "comfort food" along with crusty bread to soak up all the extra braising liquid.

Ingredients:

- 5 pounds beef short ribs, trim excess fat
- 1 each large onion, chopped
- 2 each carrots, chopped
- 4 sticks celery, chopped
- 3 cloves garlic, peeled
- 1/4 cup tomato paste
- 1 cup beef stock
- 5 each fresh thyme sprigs
- 1 each bay leaf
- 2 cups Glenora Cabernet Sauvignon
- 1/4 cup olive oil

Pre-heat oven to 350 degrees. In a large sauce pot add oil and sear all sides of the short rib for about three minutes on each side on medium high heat. Remove ribs from pan and add onion, carrots, celery, and garlic cook for ten minutes, then add tomato paste, thyme, and bay leaf and cook for an additional five minutes. Deglaze with Cabernet Sauvignon, add the beef stock and cover. Place in oven and cook for approximately three hours or until fork-tender. Remove ribs from the sauce and strain the sauce. Pour the sauce over the ribs just before serving.

Makes six servings.

During the slow-cooking period, the meat's connective tissue and fibers melt and soften, releasing a depth of flavor and richness that is impossible to achieve using any other method.

Rosemary-Scented Lamb Chops

Rosemary's fragrant flavor, reminiscent of pine and balsam, is a traditional, dependable complement to lamb. It works wonders, not only as an infusion for the grilled chops, but as flavoring in an accompanying polenta. A branch of rosemary makes an excellent basting stick—dip in olive oil and brush over the meat.

Ingredients:

8 lamb loin chops, 6 oz each
1 cup olive oil
1 each lemon, slice
3 springs rosemary

For the rosemary polenta:

1/2 cup course corn meal
1/2 teaspoon rosemary, chopped
1 teaspoon salt
1/2 teaspoon black pepper
1-1/2 cup milk
1 cup water

Trim any excess fat of the lamb loin. Mix together the olive oil, lemon, and rosemary.

Combine all ingredients and place in refrigerator for twenty-four hours. Pre-heat grill to a medium-high heat. Remove chops from marinade and place on a lightly oiled grill rack. Grill for four minutes on each side. Remove from heat, allow to rest for five minutes before serving.

To make the polenta: place rosemary, salt, pepper, milk and water in a sauce pot. Bring ingredients to a boil. Add in cornmeal. Turn down to a simmer and cook out for about twenty minutes or until smooth, stirring occasionally. Serve hot.

Makes four servings.

According to folklore, the bright blue of rosemary's small flowers appeared only after the Virgin Mary draped her veil over the bush. From then on the herb was called Rose of Mary.

Bitter Orange-Rubbed Roast Fresh Ham

Fresh ham is simply an un-smoked, un-cured shank and leg of pork. Cabernet Sauvignon's voluptuous fruit and spice notes offer a remarkable match with the savory fresh roast and the aromatherapy of bitter oranges. The skin of the fresh ham, if properly cooked, is crisp and crunchy, a tasty tidbit to nibble on.

Ingredients:

- 1 fresh ham (12-15 lbs)
- 12 bitter oranges
- 1 garlic head, minced
- 2 tablespoon kosher salt
- 1 tablespoon ground black pepper
- 1 teaspoon ground oregano

Score the outer skin of the ham in a diamond pattern. Mix the orange, garlic, salt, pepper, and oregano together. Rub marinade into ham and let marinate for twenty-four hours. Cook in a 325-degree oven for four to five hours or until internal temperature reaches 165 degrees. Let rest for half an hour before serving.

Makes twelve servings.

It's not surprising that bitter orange rub adds such a wonderful fragrance to this dish. The extract of bitter oranges is a common ingredient in many perfumes.

Cabernet Franc

Asking a winemaker which is the favorite is like asking a parent to single out a favorite child. Steve has his favorites, but he isn't saying. About Cabernet Franc he does say that this is a cold-hardy red grape and a later ripening one, which is both good and bad. It means having to leaf thin, to provide optimum sun exposure for the long ripening grapes, and that means having to compete with birds (birds seem to like the grapes that are the most expensive to produce).

Toward the latter part of the season, what the birds don't cluster-thin for him, Steve usually has to finish.

The Cabernet Franc comes from two vineyards and although they are only hundreds of yards apart, the fruit of their respective vines is often quite different. Steve usually makes the wines of each vineyard separately and then blends them later on, after he evaluates their development in the wine cellar. One lot might need less oak aging than the other and so on.

The one thing he is extra careful about is Cabernet Franc's reaction to the vintage: in some years, the grape can produce a green pepper aroma and taste. This is the result of a combination of natural components in the grape that may not have had enough time to fully develop. Steve says that just 1% of the whole crop with the green pepper forwardness can affect the whole lot of wine. It's one more reason he keeps wine from separate vineyards apart until the very end.

The result of Steve's treatment of Cabernet Franc shows in the almost meaty aroma of the wine, its unusually viscous body (for a cool climate grape) and its overall tannin intensity. Cabernet Franc does well paired with red meats, but it does even better next to meats like game with deep, rich texture.

WINE CELLAR STORIES

Cabernet Franc is a major grape in Bordeaux, but also in the northern cool Loire region of France as well as in the cool regions of northeastern Italy. It's a cinch in the Finger Lakes.

Chicken and Lentil Soup

This delicious and hearty winter soup starts with a classic mirepoix, an old-fashioned mixture of diced garlic, onion, carrot and celery softened by gentle cooking. Cabernet Franc is the recommended accompaniment, the same wine used to spike the broth. The wine provides robust interest and its powerful fruit harmonizes with the slightly peppery lentils.

Ingredients:

1/2 pound green lentils, cooked
6 cups chicken stock
1 small onion
2 small carrots, small dice
1 stick celery, small dice
2 cloves garlic, minced
6 ounces chicken breast, julienne
2 tablespoon fresh thyme leaves
1/2 cup Glenora Cabernet Franc
1 tablespoon lemon juice
2 tablespoons salt
1 tablespoon ground black pepper
1 bay leaf

In a medium pot, cook onion until translucent. Add the garlic and cook for three minutes, then add carrots and celery and cook for five minutes. Add the chicken, thyme, and bay leaf; cook for five minutes then add the wine, lemon juice, salt and pepper. Simmer for three minutes, then add the chicken stock and lentils and simmer for an additional thirty minutes. Serve hot.

Makes four servings.

Dark green French lentils, or lentilles du Puy, are more intensely flavored and a bit sweeter than the more earthy, "dull" green lentils. They hold their shape well after cooking and are excellent in both soups and salads.

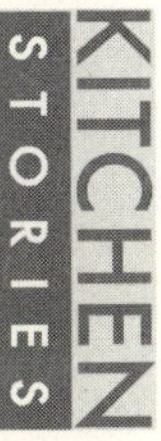

Steak and Blue Cheese Salad

When paired with steak, Cabernet Franc comes alive with a burst of fruit and a complexity that stands up to the most flavorful of dishes. This entrée salad combines the rich taste and texture of sirloin, salty-tart blue cheese, sweet cherry tomatoes and earthy beets to create a dish with dizzying layers of depth.

Ingredients:

1 pound salad greens
4 4-ounce sirloin steaks
4 large red beets
1 pint cherry tomatoes
1 ounce red wine vinegar
3 ounces olive oil
1/2 red onion, small dice
4 ounces blue cheese
To taste salt
To taste ground black pepper

Season steak with salt, pepper and rub the outside with a little olive oil. Grill steak to desired temperature and reserve. Place beets in a pre-heated, 375-degree oven on a sheet pan. Roast in oven for an approximately one hour. Take out and let cool. Peel and slice thin. In a small bowl mix together salt, black pepper, red wine vinegar, olive oil and red onion. Place beet on bottom of plate and drizzle dressing on top. Mix the salad greens with one ounce of the dressing; place on top of beets. Slice steak and place around salad and finish with blue cheese and cherry tomatoes.

Makes four servings.

KITCHEN STORIES

Bergere Bleue is a Roquefort-style, sheep's milk cheese produced at Northland Farm in Marathon. This moist and slightly crumbly cheese, aged for up to one year, achieves a spicy piquancy from the blue-green streaks of Penicillium roquefortii.

"Reuben Meets Rachel" Sandwich

In this version of the deli original, pastrami replaces traditional corned beef (making it a "Rachel"), keeping the standard sauerkraut, and upgrading the Russian dressing. Muranda Farms provides a local connection with "Red Buddy" cheese, a hybrid of Swiss and Gouda styles. While Dr. Brown's Cel-Ray soda may be the expected pairing, be adventurous—try it with a glass of Cabernet Franc.

Ingredients:

8 slices rye bread
1/2 cup sauerkraut
12 ounces pastrami, thinly sliced
1/2 pound Red Buddy cheese
1/4 pound unsalted butter
4 tablespoons Russian dressing

For the Russian dressing:

1/2 lemon, juiced
2 gherkins
1 small shallot
1 teaspoon capers
1 cup mayonnaise
1 teaspoon paprika
1 tablespoon ketchup
1 teaspoon red wine vinegar
To taste salt and pepper

To make the dressing: in a food processor add juice of half a lemon, gherkins, half of the shallot, garlic and capers. Pulse until finely chopped. Fold in with mayonnaise, paprika, ketchup and vinegar; season with a little salt and pepper to taste.

In a non-stick pan melt two tablespoons of butter and place four slices of bread down. Place two slices of cheese on each piece of the bread; place one tablespoon of dressing on top of the cheese, then a thin layer of sauerkraut. Top each piece of bread with about three ounces of pastrami, then another slice of bread. Cook sandwiches on both sides until bread achieves a golden light brown color.

Makes four servings.

The Reuben sandwich is one of New York City's contributions to the world of eating, invented, according to Craig Claiborne, by Arthur Reuben, owner of Reuben's Delicatessen, around 1914.

Latin Spice-Rubbed Filet Mignon with Herbed Spaghetti Squash

Cumin, coriander and paprika infuse the tender beef with fragrant spices common to Latin cuisine. One of the great advantages of filet mignon is that it absorbs bold flavors yet still maintains its meaty personality throughout the cooking process. Cabernet Franc finds a wonderful alchemy with the complexity of flavors.

Ingredients:

4 6-ounce filets mignon
2 tablespoon olive oil
1 teaspoon cumin
1 teaspoon coriander
1 teaspoon paprika
1 teaspoon salt
1/2 teaspoon ground black pepper
For the spaghetti squash:
1 large spaghetti squash
1 teaspoon chives, finely chopped
1 teaspoon rosemary, finely chopped
1 teaspoon thyme leaves, finely chopped
2 tablespoons unsalted butter
To taste salt
To taste ground black pepper

Preheat oven to 350 degrees. Place a skillet on medium high heat. Mix together the cumin, coriander, paprika, salt, and black pepper. Rub the outside of the filet with the spice and oil. Place filet in skillet and sear each side for two minutes, then place in oven and cook to desired temperature.

Preheat oven to 350 degrees. Cut the squash lengthwise and scoop out the seeds. Place on a sheet pan open face down, cover the bottom of the pan with water and place in oven for about one hour. Remove squash from oven, and with a fork scrape out the squash and set aside. In a saute pan place the butter and let melt, then add squash, thyme, rosemary and chives to pan. Stir together and cook for about five minute or until hot throughout. Season with salt and pepper before serving.

Makes four servings.

When raw, the flesh of spaghetti squash (or calabash squash) is solid and similar to other raw squash; when cooked, the flesh falls away from the fruit in strands that look just like spaghetti noodles.

Fiddleheads and Greens with Dried-Cherry Vinaigrette

The tart/sweet of dried cherries softens the nutty, slightly bitter bite of fiddlehead ferns, one of spring's most elusive greens. Harvested locally for only a few weeks in April, fiddleheads taste a bit like asparagus and artichoke, as they take center stage in a salad of locally-picked watercress and baby lolla rosa with the pleasing crunch of toasted almonds. Pairing with the ripe fruit of Cabernet Franc takes the experience up another notch.

Ingredients:

- 1 cup fiddlehead ferns (boiled for 10 minutes)
- 8 ounces watercress
- 4 ounces baby lolla rosa
- 1 ounce toasted, sliced almonds
- 1 ounce red wine vinegar
- 1 ounce Glenora Cabernet Franc
- 3 ounces almond oil
- 4 ounces olive oil
- 1 lemon, juiced
- 1-1/4 ounce dried cherries

Combine the vinegar, wine, almond oil and lemon juice. Whisk in the olive oil gradually. Add the dried cherries and season with salt and pepper to taste. Set dressing a side and reserve. Rinse the fiddleheads under cold water, cut off the bottom end piece, and blanch in boiling water for about 1 minute. Pat dry with a paper towel. Wash and spin dry the watercress and lolla rosa; take off any blemished greens. Assemble salad by tossing lolla rosa, watercress, and fiddle head ferns together with the vinaigrette. Serve on salad plates; sprinkle toasted almonds on top.

Makes four servings.

KITCHEN STORIES

The young fiddlehead is a type of fern that hasn't yet "unfurled" and opened its leaves. Its end is tightly coiled, wrapped around tiny budding leaves. As the name suggests, the fern frond looks like the spiral end of a violin.

MERLOT

It's mellifluous, it's well known, and despite the movie, *Sideways*, Merlot is a fantastic grape variety. But it isn't an easy one to grow in the Finger Lakes. To do that takes passion, commitment, and ingenuity; no, make that flexibility.

Not only are Merlot vines rather tender during winter they are also later ripening in autumn. In the Finger Lakes region, late ripening can mean exposure to early frost. What that means to Steve is overseeing cluster thinning for good sun exposure, while keeping a watchful eye on the weather.

Leaf thinning might follow cluster thinning for optimum sun exposure throughout the growing season. Sun is critical so that the grapes can reach 'veraison'—the point where their skins turn red—at the right time in the growing cycle to make sure the crop is ready on time, before any threat of early frost.

After the grapes are harvested, heat management continues during skin fermentation, a critical step to maintain color and intensity. The fermenting vats are carefully scrutinized to see how much pumping over or punching down the cap is required, and when, to both cool down the rising temperature and to circulate an even color throughout the wine.

Finally, the wine is softened through a secondary fermentation called malolactic, as it converts the wine's natural malic acid into the milder lactic acid to round out the flavors.

The hallmark of the way Steve treats Merlot is the wine's dark cherry fruit quality plus its velvet-like finish, despite the intense tannins.

Merlot is a natural for lamb, grilled vegetables (especially eggplant) and mushrooms.

WINE CELLAR STORIES

In the movie, Sideways, *the main character spends most of his time seeking what he thinks is the greatest wine of all, and it isn't Merlot. He raves about the beauty of a French wine called Cheval Blanc, which happens to about 50% Merlot.*

Breast of Duck Salad with Wild Rice and Bulgar Wheat

The contrast of earthy grains and tender duck is delicious, with currants soaked in Merlot adding an unexpected note. Fruit-forward Merlot exquisitely matches the richness of the meat. Duck breast eats more like steak than chicken and is slightly pink in the center when properly cooked.

Ingredients:

2 duck breasts, 6 ounces
1 cup bulgur wheat, cooked
1/2 cup wild rice, cooked
3 tablespoon red wine vinegar
1 tablespoon virgin olive oil
1/4 cup black currants, soaked in one cup of Glenora Merlot, for one hour
To taste salt and pepper

Dry the duck breast of any moisture and score the skin with a knife. In a large, heavy-duty skillet over low heat, render skin side down for about eight minutes, then place in a 350-degree oven for about six minutes. Remove and set aside. Mix the wild rice, bulgur wheat, vinegar, currants and olive oil together; season with salt and pepper. Place rice in center of plate. Thinly slice duck breast with the skin side up and arrange around the rice.

Makes four servings.

KITCHEN STORIES

Wild rice is not true rice but rather a cereal grass harvested in shallow water along the shores of streams and lakes. Sometimes called "Indian rice," it was once a staple in the diet of Native American tribes in the Midwest.

Chicken Capellini with Plum Tomato-Caper Sauce

Garlic-seasoned chicken combines with earthy, slightly smoky tomatoes and piquant, salty capers in a Merlot-spiked pasta dish that is not only robust and flavorful, it's also quick and easy to make. The wine's supple, sweet fruit characters match up just right, like adding woodwinds to the strings of an orchestra.

Heat a sauce pan on medium-high heat, then add olive oil. Lightly toast the garlic; add the chicken and cook for about two minutes on each side. Add capers, Merlot, and lemon juice and let simmer for three minutes. Add tomatoes, salt, pepper and fresh basil. Let simmer for about ten minutes, then add the cooked pasta. Finish by adding salt and pepper to taste. Plate and serve hot with shaved parmesan cheese over the top.

Makes four servings.

Ingredients:

1/2 pound capellini pasta
1 pound chicken breast, 1/4-inch strips
32 ounces plum tomatoes, crushed
1 teaspoon capers
1 ounce fresh basil leaves, chopped
2 teaspoons minced garlic
1 juiced lemon
1 tablespoon virgin olive oil
1/4 cup Glenora Merlot
To taste salt
To taste black pepper
1/2 cup shaved parmesan cheese

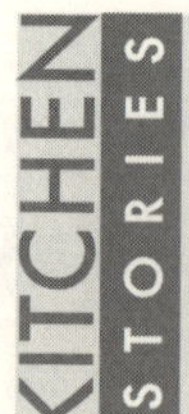

Native to the Mediterranean, capers are harvested by hand, selected for roundness and firmness. Once cured in vinegar brine or salt, they develop salty, sour and herbal flavors.

Merlot-and-Tomato Lamb Stew

The hearty lamb stew, full of potatoes, onions, peas and carrots, gets a real boost of flavor from rich, fruit-driven Merlot. Since the cooking process will evaporate and reduce liquids, the wine's essence and aromatics concentrate and intensify. Sipping the same wine alongside a bowl of stew completes the sensory experience.

Ingredients:

- 3 pounds lamb stew meat, large dice
- 2 cups beef stock
- 1 cup Glenora Merlot
- 2 tomatoes, seeded and small diced
- 2 garlic cloves, minced
- 1 fresh thyme leaves
- 1 bay leaf
- 6 red bliss potatoes, quartered length wise
- 2 carrots, obliqued cut
- 12 pearl onions, peeled
- 1/2 cup green peas, shelled and blanched
- 3 tablespoons olive oil

In a large stock pot, add oil and sear the lamb on medium-high heat. Add garlic, bay leaf and pearl onion and cook for about three minutes. Add the beef stock and Merlot. Cook in pre-heated oven for one hour at 350 degrees. Remove from oven and add in the potatoes, carrots, fresh thyme and tomatoes. Stir all together. Return to oven and cook for another hour or until lamb is tender. Just before removing from oven, add the peas for about five minutes.

Makes six servings.

Throughout the ages, wine and wine grapes have been used in cooking. Romans prepared a concentrate of unfermented grape juice called defrutum both to color and sweeten foods.

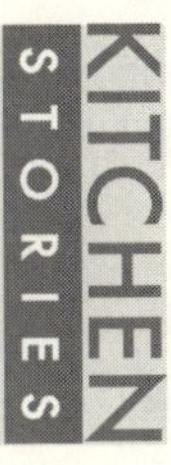

Merlot-Braised Cipollini Onions

Braised onions are the side of choice with the Lamb Stew (recipe on page 109), but they are also wonderful with roast beef dishes. Italian onions that arrive in late summer, Cipollinis have more residual sugar than white or yellow onions; braising caramelizes the sugars and makes them even sweeter.

Ingredients:
16 cipollini onions, peeled
1 cup Glenora Merlot
2 tablespoon vegetable oil
1 teaspoon salt
1/4 teaspoon black pepper

Pre-heat oven to 350 degrees. Peel the outer skin of the cipollini onions. Place a sauté pan with vegetable oil on medium high-heat and add the onions. Cook until golden brown. Add salt, pepper and Merlot. Place the pan in the oven for about twenty minutes or until the onions become tender.

Makes four servings.

KITCHEN STORIES

To peel the onions easily, cut off the ends, place in a pot of boiling water. Blanch for one minute and drain. The outer peel will slip off when you squeeze the onions.

SYRAH

You know that game when someone says a word or phrase and you must respond quickly with the first thing that comes into your mind?

Let's play. I'll say Shiraz or Syrah (it is the same grape) and you'll say…

Well, you wouldn't be wrong, but you would be missing something. The next time someone says to you either Shiraz or Syrah, say Finger Lakes right back.

Why Syrah in the Finger Lakes, you ask?

Because one of the Glenora partners, Scott Welliver, happens to love the variety—he also happens to be the grape grower who planted the vines at Norbud Farm, that provide the winery with Syrah. These vineyards are on the east side of Seneca, in that grape growing area we've told you about that is affectionately known as "the banana belt," which, if it weren't a decidedly warm spot, likely could not give us these rich, tannic Syrah grapes.

In autumn, when the grapes ripen, Syrah grapevine leaves might look like fall colors on overdrive. That's because the variety is especially prone to a disease called leaf roll, which curls the leaves and turns them red. Unfortunately, the vine's canopy also loses leaves during harvest, making the red grapes perfect targets for fruit-loving birds. Picking Syrah is a race to the finish line between harvesters and birds.

In many ways, however, leaf roll is a friendly disease; it gives that bright red color to the leaves and it also reduces the vine's vegetative vigor, which is exactly what a cool growing region needs to focus intensity in the longer maturing red grapes like Syrah.

When you sniff the finished Syrah wine, you might sneeze from the whiff of black pepper common to this variety. That pepper is accompanied by a lighter-bodied but no less tannic red that can—and must—stand up against big dishes that include Pekin duck, beef carpaccio, and big vegetables like butternut squash. The adventuresome among us might like Syrah with spiced sausages or maybe meatballs!

WINE CELLAR STORIES

Legend has it that the Shiraz grape originates in the Southern Persian city of the same name—recent DNA research proves otherwise. The grape is an offshoot of two relatively obscure grape varieties: Mondeuse Blanche and Dureza.

Beef Carpaccio

In pairing food and wine, the goal is synergy and balance. When the fine bright acids of the Syrah are matched with the high-acid balsamic vinegar in this preparation, the acidities tend to cancel each other out, allowing the ripe fruit in the wine to come through. Carpaccio has a delicate texture, in perfect balance with the supple tannins of the Syrah.

Ingredients:

8 ounces beef tenderloin, all fat trimmed off
1 ounce extra virgin olive oil
1 ounce balsamic vinegar
1 ounce capers
1/2 small red onion, minced

Season the outside of the beef with salt and pepper. Heat the oil over high heat and sear the beef on all sides. Remove and let cool. Wrap tight in plastic wrap and freeze until it becomes solid and easy to slice very thin with a sharp knife or a electric slicer. Arrange the meat on plate and add capers and onions and drizzle with balsamic and extra virgin olive oil.

Makes four servings.

KITCHEN STORIES

The dish was named "Carpaccio" by Giuseppe Cipriani, owner of Harry's Bar in Venice, because the colors of the dish reminded him of paintings by the Venetian painter Vittore Carpaccio.

Roast
Pekin Duck

The distinctive flavor of duck simply begs for the rich, intensely-flavored Syrah with its shades of cherry, black pepper, and spicy finish. The duck is enriched with some of the fat from beneath the bird's skin during roasting; the skin becomes perfectly crisp while the meat is juicy and superbly tender.

Ingredients:
2 whole Pekin ducks
4 garlic cloves
6 sprigs thyme
6 sprigs rosemary
To taste salt
To taste pepper

Pre-heat oven to 400 degrees. Remove the gizzard and neck from the inside of the duck. Trim off the excess fat from the neck part of the duck. Season the outside of the ducks with salt and pepper, then season the inside cavities: distribute the garlic, thyme and rosemary between both birds. Put the duck in a roasting pan and place in oven for approximately forty-five minutes. Remove from the oven let rest for about fifteen minutes before carving.

Makes four servings.

KITCHEN STORIES

In 1873, nine domesticated Pekin ducks were exported from China to Long Island, New York, for breeding. Farmers realized that the south shore was perfect for raising ducks, and today the "Long Island duckling" is the most popular commercial duck breed in America.

Spaghetti and Buffalo Meatballs

A humble dish of spaghetti and meatballs, when transformed with the sweet, subtle gaminess of buffalo meat and tangy, nutty flavor of kefir cheese, offers a satisfying partner with the dark fruit flavors of Syrah.

Ingredients:

For the meatballs:

1-1/2 pounds buffalo meat, ground
2 ounces kefir cheese, grated (Finger Lakes Dexter Creamery)
12 kalamata olives, small dice
2 egg yolks
1/4 cup bread crumbs
1/2 teaspoon minced garlic
1 tablespoon kosher salt
1 teaspoon black pepper

For the pasta:

1 pound spaghetti
6 quarts water
1 tablespoon salt
2 tablespoon olive oil

For the sauce:

32 ounces crushed tomatoes
1 ounce fresh basil leaves, chopped
2 teaspoon minced garlic
1 tablespoon virgin olive oil
1/4 cup Glenora Syrah
Salt, to taste
Black pepper, to taste

To make the meatballs: in a mixing bowl, mix all meatball ingredients together. Form into one-ounce meatballs. Place onto a sheet pan and cook in a 375-degree oven for fifteen minutes. Remove from oven and set aside.

To make the pasta: add the salt and oil to the water in a large pot and bring to a boil. Add the pasta and cook for ten minutes. Strain and set aside.

To make the sauce: add oil to a sauce pan over medium-high heat. Add the garlic and lightly toast. Add the Syrah, and fresh basil. Let simmer for about ten minutes. Add the cooked pasta and buffalo meatballs. Season with salt and pepper to taste. Plate and serve hot with some grated kefir cheese on top.

Makes four servings.

KITCHEN STORIES

Each wheel of local kefir cheese is handcrafted from creamy, raw milk of the grass-fed and pastured Irish Dexter cows at Finger Lakes Dexter Creamery on the east side of Cayuga Lake.

Butternut Squash Puree

Think of this rich puree as a more adventurous alternative to a side of mashed potatoes. Butternut squash has a bulbous end and pale, creamy skin, with a choice, fine-textured, deep-orange flesh. Its sweet, nutty, full flavor is somewhat similar to sweet potatoes, a rich counterpart to the robust Syrah.

Ingredients:
- 2 butternut squash
- 1/4 pound unsalted butter
- To taste salt
- To taste black pepper

Peel the squash, then cut in half lengthwise and deseed. Rough-chop the butternut squash and place in a pot. Cover the squash with water one inch above the butternut and let simmer for approximately forty-five minutes or until fork tender. Brown the butter in a sauté pan. Strain the butternut and place in a food processor with the brown butter and puree to a smooth consistency. Season with salt and pepper.

Makes four servings.

Squash was one of the "Three Sisters" (along with maize and beans) planted by Native Americans, considered such an important part of the diet that they buried it with their dead to provide nourishment for the final journey.

Meritage

Contrary to what your French 101 instructor might say, Meritage rhymes with heritage. That's because Meritage is a made-up English word to identify a certain wine classification that relies on blending.

If Steve had his way, he'd produce a much greater volume of Cabernet Sauvignon wine. But in the Finger Lakes, the winemaker works for the weather. Cabernet Sauvignon needs an extended growing season, and so it can be problematic—and that's why the wine gods invented blending.

Meritage is always a blended red wine composed of two or more from the Cabernet Sauvignon, Cabernet Franc, and Merlot grapes, commonly called the Bordeaux grape varieties because they were made famous in that French wine region hundreds of years ago.

Because of the blend, this wine is unlike your regular cool climate red. It gets its intensity first from Steve's meticulous cluster thinning right after veraison (that time of year when the grape skins begin to turn to red).

By thinning the clusters, Steve removes the immature grapes and he also increases the sun exposure and available plant sugar to the grapes for good ripening. To accomplish this grape cluster control Steve and the vineyard crew must travel to a number of vineyards that span from the west shore of Seneca Lake to its east shore and then to Cayuga Lake, for those are the many places where the grapes for this wine are grown.

After fermentation, the wine's intensity is increased through aging in French and American oak for as many months as constant tasting proves necessary.

In the end, Meritage is a wine with the tastes of dark red fruits and the power of tannin—perfect for fatty foods like sharp cheeses, red meats, and mocha.

WINE CELLAR STORIES

Meritage is a trademarked organization of wine producers who pay a membership fee for use of the name. When Meritage *is on the label, the American wine must have been produced from the classic Bordeaux grape varieties and no other.*

Celeriac Salad with Blue Cheese

This Meritage-friendly dish includes an elegant symphony of flavors—buttery, salty, sweet, juicy, fruity, and earthy—complementing the complexity of the wine. Blue cheese partners well with assertive root vegetables, accenting the bracing character of celery root. This salad is delicious on its own, as part of a composed salad, or as a sort of relish accompaniment to roast meats.

Ingredients:

4 ounces blue cheese (Lively Run Cayuga Blue)
1 celeriac, peeled and thinly sliced
8 dates, seeded and quartered
1 orange, juice and zest
3/4 cup olive oil
1 tablespoon lemon juice

Season celeriac, and date with salt and pepper to taste. Mix with olive oil, lemon juice, zest, and orange juice together with celeriac mixture and plate up. Sprinkle about one ounce of blue cheese on each salad.

Makes four servings.

"Cayuga Blue" gets its minty, lightly spicy flavors from the milk of Lively Run Goat Dairy's herd of 120 floppy-eared Nubians and rabbit-eared Alpines.

Grilled Filet Mignon with Shallot-Red Wine Sauce

The blend of wine varieties in Meritage presents a flavor profile of greater strength and complexity than its single components would exhibit standing alone. Since the flavor of filet mignon tends to be mild, we prefer to serve it with a flavorful sauce. The rule of thumb for cooking with wine is to use a good wine, something you would be happy drinking, so what better ingredient for the sauce than the wine you will be serving at the table.

Ingredients:

4 filet mignon steaks, 8-ounce portions
2 shallots
4 ounces Glenora Port
4 ounces Glenora Meritage
2 teaspoons fresh thyme leaves
2 ounces heavy cream
2 teaspoons lemon juice
2 teaspoons olive oil
To taste salt and pepper

Grill filet mignon to your doneness preference. In a small saute pan add olive oil and shallots cook for five minutes over a medium-high heat. Add thyme, Port and Meritage; let simmer until reduced by half. Add lemon juice, heavy cream, salt and pepper. Simmer for two minutes and serve over steak.

Makes four servings.

KITCHEN STORIES

One of the pleasures of cooking with a good wine is having a glass alongside, so you may reward your efforts in the kitchen with a sip from time to time.

Sirloin Steak Wrap

The bold complexity of Meritage suggests a dish that challenges the palate with a forthright bit of heat. The wine dances to a lively Latin beat alongside paprika-rubbed slices of sirloin steak and tortilla stuffings, complementing the earthy, mineral characters in the wine.

Heat a large sauté pan until very hot. Rub the steak with olive oil, paprika, salt and pepper. Cook to desired temperature and reserve.

Mix the arugula with the tomatoes, lemon juice, and olive oil. Wipe out sauté pan; heat tortillas in pan on medium heat, one at a time until warm. Remove from heat and lay warm tortillas flat on table. On each tortilla, place sliced steak, salad, hummus, and sour cream. Tightly roll each tortilla around filling ingredients, pressing with hands to maintain shape.

Makes four servings.

Ingredients:

1-1/2 pounds sirloin steak
4 teaspoons paprika
8 ounces arugula
8 tablespoons hummus
4 tablespoons sour cream
4 vine-ripened tomatoes
2 lemons, juiced
2 tablespoons olive oil
4 tortilla wraps
To taste salt and pepper

KITCHEN STORIES

Nothing tastes like summer as much as tomatoes that are allowed to ripen on the vine before they're picked. These wonderfully fragrant tomatoes add sweet, zesty flavor to the dish.

Roasted Garlic Beef Stew

A long, slow simmer in the hearty red wine helps to tenderize the beef in this Finger Lakes Wine Country version of French boeuf bourguignon, classically flavored with red Burgundy. In our interpretation, garlic adds another flavor layer to the broth of the stew, enriched with local vegetables and a robust Glenora Meritage that stands up to the long cooking.

Ingredients:

- 1-1/2 pounds boneless beef shank, cut into large 2-inch pieces
- 1 tablespoon kosher salt
- 1 teaspoon black pepper, ground
- 2 ounces olive oil
- 1 large Spanish onion, small dice
- 8 cloves garlic, roasted
- 1 ounce tomato paste
- 1 cup Glenora Meritage
- 32 ounces beef stock
- 1 bay leaf
- 4 sprigs fresh thyme
- 3 sprigs fresh rosemary
- 1/2 pound carrots, peeled and medium dice
- 1/2 pound turnips, peeled and medium dice
- 12 pearl onions, peeled

Season the beef with salt and pepper. Heat the oil over medium-high heat in a braiser, then sear all the meat until deep brown on all sides. Remove from pot and set aside. Add onion and cook until translucent. Add garlic and tomato paste and cook for one minute. Add the Meritage wine and let simmer for three minutes. Add bay leaf, thyme, rosemary, beef stock and the seared beef. Cover and place in oven at 325 degrees for one hour. Remove from the oven, skim off excess fat; add in the carrots, turnips, and pearl onions. Return to the oven and cook for an additional hour or until fork tender. Remove from the oven and take out herb stems and bay leaf before serving.

Makes four servings.

Boeuf bourguignon is an example of French culinary incongruity. While it is a peasant food made with tough cuts of beef and leftover vegetables, the stew is usually served with the world's most noble wines.

Mocha Cheesecake

Red wine and chocolate seem to be a darling pair these days. With its deep, dark cocoa/mocha layers, the noble Meritage Bordeaux blend suggests the adventurous pairing with a rich dessert like cheesecake. The wine's tannins mellow the sweetness and cut through the rich flavors, preparing your palate for the next bite.

To make the crust: combine all ingredients in bowl and mix well. Put mixture into a twelve-inch tart pan. Press firmly into bottom and sides of pan. Bake for ten minutes in a 350-degree oven. Remove from oven and set aside.

To make the filling: combine all ingredients except the chocolate in a food processor and blend until smooth. Pour mixture into the crust. Drizzle the melted chocolate over the top. Bake in pre-heated 300-degree oven for forty-five minutes or until a toothpick inserted into the center comes out clean.

Makes eight servings.

Ingredients:

For the crust:

1 cup chocolate graham crackers, ground
1 cup graham crackers
1 cup light brown sugar
2 ounces melted butter

For the filling:

1-1/2 pounds cream cheese
3/4 cup granulated sugar
1-1/2 ounces espresso, cooled
3 eggs, large
1/4 cup heavy cream
1/4 cup all-purpose flour
Pinch salt
1 ounce coffee liqueur
2 ounces semi-sweet chocolate, melted

The flavors of chocolate and coffee unite so naturally and seamlessly, it reminds us that the world is still full of magic.

Special Occasion Wines & Recipes

SPARKLING WINE

Without doubt, the Finger Lakes region is among the premier sparkling wine-producing regions of the world. That's because it takes bracingly crisp acidity to make fine sparkling wine, and that takes a cool climate-growing region like ours.

Our Brut Sparkling Wine is produced the old-fashioned way: with painstaking human labor to guide every facet of the operation, from selecting and picking the best grapes to turning the bottles one-quarter clockwise every so often to allow yeast cells to settle as the wine ages, to disgorging the base wine before bottling the finished product, and to capping it with a wire tight seal to keep in the effervescence—it's all done by hand.

The blend is 60/40, Pinor Noir/Chardonnay, the classic blending grapes in the French Champagne region. Along with this varietal blend of the Champagne region, we employ the winemaking system that was perfected in Champagne hundreds of years ago. (At times, when the vintage is just right, we produce Blanc de Blanc sparkling wine from only Chardonnay grapes.)

After producing a low alcohol still wine from the two products we blend what is referred to as the "cuvée," bottle it, and then re-ferment the wine in the bottle; there it builds a yeasty backbone and racks up millions of tiny bubbles of carbon dioxide.

When the wine is finished, and the yeast is settled out, we release the yeast cells by disgorging them from the bottle and quickly top up the bottle to make up for the lost volume; then, we cork it and apply the wire capping to contain the carbon dioxide pressure.

It takes from 24 to 36 months to produce a finished Glenora sparkling wine and then, it is capped and ready for release.

Most think of sparkling wine for festive occasions like holidays and birthdays, but it is among the most food-friendly wines of all. Sparkling wine is a perfect starter with the appetizer, a marvelous foil for a variety of main courses, and a welcome palate cleanser between the main course and dessert.

WINE CELLAR STORIES

Some refer to any sparkling wine as Champagne. *We don't think that is fair to the people of the French region named Champagne, where the wine was created in the 18th century. We call it* Sparkling Wine, *and we produce it in the Méthode Champenoise (Champagne Method).*

Parmesan Cheese Stick Wrapped with Prosciutto

An ideal evening of entertaining begins with a flute of Sparkling Wine and passed appetizers. On a tray of hors d'oeuvres, this supreme interpretation of the ham and cheese partnership is certain to take center stage. You could hardly ask for more in terms of flavor than sweet, salty prosciutto paired with fruity, nutty parmesan. The crisp, refreshing Glenora sparkler cleanses the palate, making a perfect and simple coupling.

Ingredients:

1 egg yolk
1 tablespoon water
1 sheet puff pastry sheet
1 ounce Reggiano parmesan, grated
12 thin slices of Prosciutto
1 ounce olive oil
1/4 cup chives, finely chopped

In a mixing bowl, mix together the egg yolk and water. Brush the puff pastry with the egg wash. Sprinkle the parmesan cheese on top. Cut into quarter-inch strips, twist and place on a parchment-lined sheet pan and bake in a 400-degree oven for ten minutes. Remove from the oven and allow to cool. Once the cheese sticks are cooled, wrap with the prosciutto. Dip each end in olive oil and coat with chives.

Makes six servings.

KITCHEN STORIES

Prosciutto is made by rubbing and massaging the hind legs of pork with an amount of salt proportionate to the weight of the meat. After the ham has been salted, it is washed, dried and left to age in aging rooms for 10 to 12 months.

Smoked Salmon with Crème Fraîche

Sparking wine is a celebratory drink, an exceptionally accommodating companion to the refined finger foods of an elegant soiree. Smoked salmon with a dollop of crème fraîche and a sprig of fresh dill is certain to impress guests, especially with a Glenora bubbly. The crisp, refreshing wine provides classic counterpoint to salty, smoky salmon. Make the crème fraîche and prepare the salmon ahead of time. Assemble just before guests arrive.

Ingredients:

1 English cucumber, sliced in 1/4 inch rounds
3 ounces smoked salmon, finely julienned
1/2 teaspoon fresh dill, chopped
1/4 cup crème fraiche
1 pinch salt
1 pinch ground black pepper

Mix the crème fraiche with the dill, salt, and pepper. Arrange the cucumber at the bottom with a teaspoon of smoked salmon, then top with a small dollop of the cream fraiche and chopped dill.

Makes six servings.

The traditional Native American method of smoking over carefully tended alderwood fires enhances the natural savory flavor of salmon.

Shucked Oysters with Sparkling Wine Vinaigrette

Sparkling wine is a perfect foil for the briny, salty creaminess of fresh oysters, lifting the oyster taste off the palate so you can start fresh with each bite. To properly shuck oysters, use a good-quality oyster knife (one with a sturdy blade that won't bend easily) and a pair of garden-type gloves to protect your hands from cuts and abrasions. The vinaigrette may be served on side or over the oysters.

Ingredients:

- 24 fresh oysters, shucked
- 1 ounce white wine vinegar
- 2-1/2 ounces olive oil
- 1/2 ounce Glenora Sparkling Brut
- 1 pinch salt
- 1/4 teaspoon course-ground black pepper

In a mixing bowl mix together the vinegar, salt, and pepper. Wisk the oil in a steady stream, then add in the sparkling wine.

Makes four servings.

To the French poet Léon-Paul Fargue, eating an oyster was "like kissing the sea on the lips." For James Beard, they were simply "one of the supreme delights that nature has bestowed on man."

Farfalle with Smoked Salmon Cream Sauce

In this rich pasta dish, the saltiness of the smoked salmon is tempered by the cream sauce. It adds a texture that perfectly frames Glenora Brut's sparkling personality. There's opportunity for maneuvering—add more or less cream to taste; use smoked trout or sturgeon instead of the salmon; serve with your favorite pasta.

Ingredients:

- 1 pound farfalle pasta, cooked
- 3 cups heavy cream
- 2 tablespoon olive oil
- 2 cloves garlic, sliced thin
- 1 shallot, minced
- 1/4 cup chives, chopped fine
- 4 ounces smoked salmon, julienned
- 1 cup parmesan cheese
- 1 cup snow peas, shelled

In a large pan over medium heat, add olive oil. Add the garlic and shallots and cook until you get a whiff of garlic. Add the heavy cream and reduce by one-third, then add the pasta. Allow the pasta to simmer in the cream for about four minutes, then add chives, peas, cheese and salmon. Stir all together for three minutes before serving.

Makes six servings.

Farfalle is often called "bow-tie pasta," its name derived from the Italian word farfalla for butterfly.

Buttermilk Fried Chicken

Marinating in buttermilk before frying gives the chicken extra flavor and keeps it moist and tender as it cooks. Just be careful to keep the oil hot enough to fry the chicken, but not hot enough to burn. Sparkling wine's acidity is balanced by the fat and savory components. Enjoy the embrace of crunchy and salty with crisp and bubbly.

Ingredients:

- 8 pieces chicken thigh and leg, poached
- 1 quart buttermilk
- 3 cups all purpose flour
- 1 teaspoon black pepper
- 1/2 teaspoon ground mace
- 1/2 teaspoon nutmeg
- 2 teaspoon kosher salt

After the chicken has been poached, drain any excess liquid. Combine the chicken and buttermilk in a large plastic bag and let soak for twenty-four hours. In a mixing bowl, mix the flour, black pepper, ground mace, nutmeg and kosher salt. Remove chicken from the buttermilk and coat with flour mixture. Re-dip into the buttermilk, then back into the flour. In a large skillet, fry four pieces of chicken in grape seed oil at 325 degrees for approximately twelve minutes or until golden brown. Remove from the skillet and set aside on paper towels to drain. Keep warm while frying the remaining chicken.

Makes four servings.

KITCHEN STORIES

As the name implies, grape seed oil comes from the seeds of grapes. It is a high smoke-point oil, which means that it gets very hot before it begins to burn, making it perfect for deep frying.

Chocolate-Covered Strawberries

Dressing fresh strawberries with a thin coating of satiny chocolate creates a glamorous pairing with sparkling wine. The wine brings out the tart juiciness of a ripe strawberry, and strawberries make the fruity undertones of the wine more readily apparent. Chocolate adds another layer of texture and a bittersweet flavor note that lingers on the tongue.

Ingredients:

1 pint strawberries
2 cups chocolate, bittersweet

Fill the bottom of a double boiler one-quarter full with water. Add the chocolate to the top of the boiler and turn the heat on high. With a rubber spatula stir the chocolate until it is fully melted, then turn off heat. Wash the strawberries and pat dry. Holding by the stem, dip each strawberry into the chocolate. As each piece is removed from the chocolate, swirl in a quick, clockwise motion to "spin" the dripping chocolate off and place on a parchment lined sheet pan. Refrigerate until ready to serve.

Makes four servings.

For "tuxedo strawberries," dip strawberries in both white and dark chocolate to create a tuxedo effect. Dip in white first, allow the chocolate to dry, then dip twice in dark chocolate to create a V of white. Buttons and a bow tie can easily be added with the tip of a toothpick.

Port Wine

The process for producing Port was developed in the 16th century near the town of Oporto, in the Douro region of Portugal. The reason behind the idea was strictly commercial: by fortifying the wine with grape brandy, Portuguese exporters and British importers were assured that the wine would make it unspoiled on ships all the way to its largest market, England.

Winemaking is both science and art, and scientists and artists always experiment.

One day, Steve left the results of an experiment on Gene Pierce's desk: a glass of Port. For a few days, whenever Steve walked by or into Gene's office, he noticed that the glass of Port still sat in the same space where he placed it.

"Hmm," Steve thought. "I guess Gene's not interested."

Then one morning, Steve noticed that the glass of Port was gone. That afternoon, Gene asked Steve if he ever thought of producing a Glenora Wine Cellars Port—and a new product was born.

Port is fortified wine. It relies on a dash of grape brandy to bring it to between 17 and 18 percent alcohol by volume. Steve begins his Port with a still wine produced from a blend of mostly vinifera wine grapes but also with a touch of seedless table grapes, for their fruitiness.

The wine is produced like any other; then the brandy is added and this blend is aged in oak. The brandy is produced from an old single-pass distilling process known as "alembic," which was developed around the 12th century in Spain when that county was under the rule of the Moors.

Today, there's another brandy-making process called the "continuous still" as opposed to the "single pass." In the latter, the alcohol in grape wine is distilled fully after numerous single passes; in the former method, the passes are treated as one long process until all the alcohol is distilled.

The single-pass method of distillation produces a more rustic, multi-leveled impression on the tongue, and is believed by many Port aficionados to be superior. It is indeed how Steve's Port tastes. The fortified wine has an earthy yet delicate mouth feel with a sweet, racy character. It is a fine partner with extra sharp blue-veined cheeses, a variety of toasted nuts, and strong bittersweet chocolates.

WINE CELLAR STORIES

Port is the wine that may have changed the way wine was bottled, from large, rounded vessels that had to be stood up on board a ship, to the long, shouldered bottle with a neck that could be stacked on its sides, thereby taking up less valuable space.

Individual Chocolate Molten Cakes with Raspberry Sauce

The sweet berry flavor and firm, powerful character of Port pair beautifully with chocolate dessert. Take a bite of this decadent cake and allow it to slowly melt on your tongue. Then sip the wine. You may never consider having one without the other again. The richest, most intensely flavored chocolates are the bittersweet darks, so intense they need the balance provided both the fruit sauce and the wine.

Ingredients:

3 whole eggs
2 egg yolks
3 ounces granulated sugar
4 ounces bittersweet chocolate, 60%
4 ounces unsalted butter
2 ounces all purpose flour
1/4 teaspoon vanilla extract

For the sauce:

1 pint raspberries
1/4 cup sugar
1/4 teaspoon vanilla extract

Butter four five-ounce ramekins and lightly coat with sugar. Place the chocolate and butter in a bowl over simmering water and melt together. Whisk the sugar, vanilla and eggs together until double in size. Add the flour and melted chocolate mix; fold together with a rubber spatula. Pour into the molds. Place the mold in freezer for twenty-four hours. To cook the molten cakes, pre-heat oven at 500 degrees and cook for fourteen minutes. Remove from oven and let sit for five minutes. Pop out of mold and serve with raspberry sauce.

To make the sauce: wash the raspberries. Place in a blender with sugar and vanilla. Blend for about 3 minutes, until smooth. Reserve in refrigerator until ready to use.

Makes four servings.

June in the Finger Lakes is raspberry season, a time when folks visit local farms for pick-your-own fresh berries right off the plant. Berries are sold by the pound and are weighed after picking right in the field.

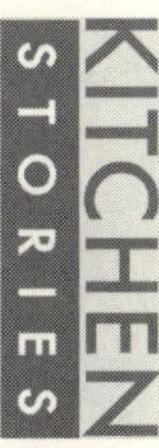

Cobbler of Rhubarb with Strawberries

Indian Run Maple Shady Farm, less than two miles from the winery, provides our kitchen with firm, crisp stalks of rhubarb, the main ingredient in this tried and true concoction. Sugar and sweet strawberries mellow the bright, tart rhubarb, and the combination counterbalances the residual sugar in Port.

Ingredients:

For the filling:

- 1 pint strawberries, washed, de-stemmed, and quartered
- 2 stalks rhubarb, washed and diced
- 1/4 cup sugar
- 1/4 teaspoon vanilla extract
- 1/4 cup unsalted butter
- 1/4 cup port wine

For the topping:

- 4 ounces unsalted butter
- 1 cup sugar
- 1 egg
- 4 ounces milk
- 1-1/2 cups flour
- 1-1/2 teaspoons baking powder
- 1/2 teaspoon baking soda
- 3/4 teaspoon salt

To make the filling: in a small pot, add the sugar, butter and vanilla and cook until melted. Add half the rhubarb and cook for about five minutes or until soft. Add the strawberries and remainder of rhubarb and cook for three more minutes. Set aside.

To make the topping: in a mixer with a paddle, cream together the butter and sugar. Add the egg and continue to mix. Add the flour, baking powder, baking soda, and salt; mix together for about one minute; add milk until incorporated (about another minute).

Place the filling into a baking dish and spread the topping over the top of the filling. Bake in a pre-heated oven at 350 degrees for twenty to thirty minutes. Test for doneness by inserting a toothpick. If it comes out clean (batter-less), it's ready to come out of the oven.

Makes four servings.

A man of many talents and interests, Ben Franklin is credited for bringing the first rhubarb seeds from England to America in 1772.

ENORA
CELLARS

Picnic Wines and Recipes

FRUIT WINES

Now that you've tried a number of our recipes on your friends and family at dinner, it's time to get out of the kitchen and into the barbecue pit—or at least on the lawn—for a picnic.

What makes a picnic so much fun is the lightness of the mood and food, for isn't that why hamburgers were invented? But hamburgers are only part of the fare for outdoor cooking, and whether under the sun or under a tree, a cool, juicy, refreshing beverage surely adds to the fun.

We offer our own versions of a picnic at the winery on the third weekend of July, August and September.

In July and August the Annual Jazz Festival comes to the Glenora Bandstand located behind the winery, featuring top-name musicians. For this event, Chef Orlando whips up his version of American classic outdoor cooking.

In September, we celebrate the coming harvest and autumn season with our Leaves and Lobsters on the lawn. The lobsters are done as all lobsters are done, in boiling water, but what goes with them matters, too, and Orlando has suggestions for that.

Winemaker Steve makes his picnic entries easy and fresh as in the pleasant and crackling Alpine White to the fruity and bright Bobsled Red wines. Plus, Steve puts forward his version of the punchbowl at your prom or wedding ceremony with a line of low alcohol fruit wines to accompany that tangy sauce on your hotdog or that hot mustard slathered over your corn on the cob.

Before you plan your family picnic, plan your picnic meal.

WINE CELLAR STORIES

Throughout history farmers have raised fruit for wines wherever grapes were scarce. Plum wine has been made in China and Japan for centuries. Apple cider and pear cider are traditional drinks in England, Sweden and France's Normandy region.

Potato Salad

Unique flavor profiles are part of the pleasure of local fingerling potatoes. Our favorite of the heirloom varieties is the Russian Banana fingerling. Its distinct buttery savor elevates the ordinary potato salad.

Ingredients:

- 1 pound 4 ounces fingerling potatoes
- 3-1/2 ounces olive oil
- 2 ounces red wine vinegar
- 2 tablespoon chopped flat leaf parsley
- 1/2 red onion, small dice
- 1 teaspoon kosher salt
- 1/4 teaspoon black pepper

Simmer the potatoes in salted water until cooked through. While the potatoes are cooking, make the dressing for the potatoes. Mix together olive oil, vinegar, parsley, red onion, salt, and black pepper. Once the potatoes are cooked, cut in quarters and mix in the dressing and let set for thirty minutes before serving.

Makes four servings.

Fingerlings are typically the size and length of a human finger, hence the name. There are many varieties, but they all tend to be low in starch with a firm, waxy texture.

Maple-Barbeque Pulled Pork

The secret to making this barbecue pulled pork recipe a mouth-watering meal is the low, slow cooking time and the sweetness and delightful depth of flavor of real maple syrup. Serve on a sliced bun as a sandwich or as the main dish of a picnic lunch or a tailgate party.

Ingredients:

- 1 pork butt (about 7 pounds), trim excess fat, and cut into 8 pieces
- 2 onions, chopped
- 2 carrots, chopped
- 3 stalks celery, chopped
- 2 tomatoes, chopped
- 1 tablespoon peppercorn
- 1 bay leaf
- 1 tablespoon dry thyme
- 2 teaspoon whole coriander
- 2 teaspoon ground cumin
- 1/8 teaspoon crushed red pepper
- 1 juniper berry
- 1 cup bourbon
- 1/4 cup cider vinegar
- 1/4 cup molasses
- 1 each chipotle pepper
- 1/4 cup New York maple syrup
- 2 cups chicken stock
- 2 cups barbeque sauce

Grill pork butt pieces on each side to make grill marks. In roasting pan, caramelize onions, then add carrots and celery. Add seasoning, and sweat for three minutes. Then add tomatoes and bourbon, then simmer for ten minutes. Add vinegar, molasses and maple syrup. Place pork over vegetables; cover and braise in oven at 325 degrees until fork-tender, or about 2-1/2 hours. Once braised, remove pork, and strain liquid. To the strained liquid add the chicken stock and BBQ sauce. Return pork back to pot and cook until pork falls apart and shreds.

Makes six servings.

New York State has a long maple history. When the first European settlers arrived in the Finger Lakes, they learned from the area's Native Americans how to tap into the trees to collect its watery sap and how to boil it down to a lush, thick syrup.

Sweet Corn and Black Bean Relish

It's not all vineyards in the Finger Lakes. There are rolling, seeming endless fields of corn, with stalks that reach up to ten feet high. Sweet corn is a picnic staple, cooked fresh on the cob or in a relish spiked with local wine.

Combine the onions, garlic, vinegar, Chardonnay, sugar, thyme, crushed red pepper, and bay leaf. Place in a medium pot and reduce until almost dry, then add corn and cook for five minutes. Finish with red pepper, and black beans. Season with salt and pepper. Serve warm or cold.

Makes six servings.

Ingredients:

6 cups fresh sweet corn kernels
1/4 pound dry black beans, soaked and cooked
2 cups onions, small dice
2 tablespoon garlic
1 cup white wine vinegar
1 cup Glenora Chardonnay
1/2 cup sugar
1 tablespoon dry thyme
1/8 teaspoon crushed red pepper
2 bay leaf
2 red pepper, small dice

KITCHEN STORIES

To enjoy the best flavor of sweet corn, it should be eaten as soon as possible after it's picked, because the precious sugars that give corn its seductive sweetness begin converting to starches as soon as the ear is off the stalk.

Spiced Chipotle Burger

Heat from chipotle and garlic changes a boring burger into something exciting, best served with a refreshing, thirst-quenching fruit wine, on the rocks or well-chilled. Canned chipotle chilies in adobo are available in your grocery store in the Mexican or "ethnic" food section.

Ingredients:

- 2 pounds ground beef
- 2 chipotle in adobo, finely chopped
- 1 teaspoon garlic minced

In a medium size mixing bowl combine all the ingredients and let marinate for and hour in the refrigerator. Make eight-ounce burger patties and grill to desired temperature.

Makes four servings.

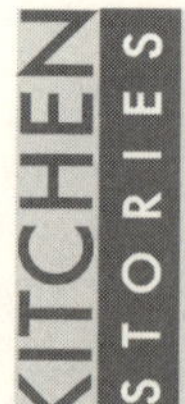

A thick slab of cheddar cheese over the top of each will take these burgers to the next level.

Grapevine-Smoked Chicken Breast

With our kitchen just steps away from the vineyard, we have a ready supply of grapevine cuttings, perfect for adding a distinctly wine country twist to chicken. Grapevines send up a nutty, slightly sweet smoke that adds subtler notes to the chicken, less overpowering than hickory or mesquite, making for a better match with most wines.

Ingredients:

- 4 chicken breasts, 6 ounces each, trimmed
- 1 pound grape vines
- 1 teaspoon kosher salt
- 1/2 teaspoon ground black pepper

Place the grapevines on the bottom of a small hotel pan and put aluminum foil on top. Poke a couple of holes in the foil with a fork. Season chicken with salt and pepper, then place on top of foil and cover. Place the pan on a burner over a low heat and smoke chicken for fifteen minutes then remove from pan. Place in oven until internal temperature reaches 165 degrees. Slice chicken and serve over a bed of greens.

Makes four servings.

As an alternative to grapevine cuttings, try smoking with chips from recycled oak wine barrels which have been used in the aging of fine wines for many years.

Southwestern Onion Rings

Not to be missed at a summertime cookout is a side order of onion rings. These thin wisps are tossed and Southwestern-accented with cornmeal and chili, begging to be enjoyed alongside a flavorful fruit wine.

Ingredients:

- 2 white onions, sliced one-quarter inch thick
- 1/2 quart heavy cream
- 2 cups all purpose flour
- 2 cups cornmeal
- 1/4 cup ancho chili powder
- 1 teaspoon kosher salt
- 1/2 teaspoon garlic powder

In a medium mixing bowl, combine the onions, and heavy cream; let sit for about one hour.

In another medium mixing bowl, mix together the flour, cornmeal, chili powder, salt and garlic. Remove onions from the cream and place in the flour mixture and toss to coat. Fry at 325 degrees, turning rings as needed, for four minutes or until golden brown. Remove the onion rings and place on a paper towel-lined plate to drain.

Makes four servings.

Cornmeal has a slightly sweet flavor that complements Vidalias or other sweet varieties of onions.

GLENORA WINE CELLARS

Recipe Index

Salads

Soup

Sandwiches

Appetizers

Pasta

Seafood

Poultry

Meat

Vegetables & Side Dishes

Desserts